Dinner and a Movie

This
short cigar
belongs to
a man with
no name.

This
long gun
belongs to
a man with
no name.

This
ponch
belongs
a man w
no nam

He's going to trigger a whole new style in adver

Dinner and a Movie

12 themed movie nights
with recipes to share & enjoy

RYLAND PETERS & SMALL
LONDON • NEW YORK

AUTHOR Katherine Bebo
DESIGN Barbara Zuñiga
EDITOR Ellen Parnavelas
PRODUCTION MANAGER Gordana Simakovic
ART DIRECTOR Leslie Harrington
EDITORIAL DIRECTOR Julia Charles

INDEXER Hilary Bird

First published in 2013
by Ryland Peters & Small
20-21 Jockey's Fields
London WC1R 4BW
and
519 Broadway, 5th Floor
New York, NY10012
www.rylandpeters.com

10 9 8 7 6 5 4 3 2 1

ISBN: 978 1 84975 441 5

A CIP record for this book is available from the British Library.

Library of Congress Cataloging-in-Publication data has been applied for.

Printed in China.

For Pops, a fellow movie buff, one-time film star (sort of) and all-round legend.

Author's Acknowledgements

Thank you to Punam Vyas for sharing your Bollywood knowledge; to Ellen Parnavelas and Julia Charles at RPS for being so great to work with, to Mum, Dad, Jonathan and Lizzie for your unrivalled love and support, to Ben for being you and, finally, to my bump who kept me company while watching countless movie clips. Can't wait to meet you, little one...

Recipe Credits

Hannah Miles pp. 10, 16, 20, 30, 40, 50, 56, 60, 70, 80, 85, 90, 100, 110, 120; Ben Reed pp. 11, 21, 31, 51, 61, 62, 71, 81, 91, 101, 111; Rachael Anne Hill and Tamsin Burnett-Hall p. 13; Jennifer Joyce pp. 14, 15, 37, 52, 53, 54, 55, 57, 115; Maxine Clark pp. 17, 23, 76; Fiona Smith p. 22; Annie Rigg pp. 24, 25, 26, 27, 36, 42, 72, 73, 74, 83, 84, 94, 95, 96, 97, 104, 107, 117; Louise Pickford p. 32; Elsa Petersen Schepelern pp. 33, 41, 44, 121; Susannah Blake pp. 34, 46, 47, 67, 77, 105; Tonia George pp. 35, 106; Linda Collister pp. 17, 43; Sonia Stevenson p. 45; Lydia France pp. 63, 65, 112; Fiona Beckett p. 64, 116; Caroline Marson pp. 66, 87; Ross Dobson p. 75; Fran Warde p. 82; Claire Burnet p. 86; Dan May p. 92; Laura Washburn p. 93; Silvana Franco p. 102; Julian Day p. 103; Sunil Vijayakar pp. 122, 123, 124, 125, 126; Clare Ferguson p. 127; Jennie Shapter p. 114.

Food Photography Credits

a= above c= centre b= below l=left r= right bk= background i= insert
Steve Baxter pp. 2 c, 5 ar, 13 a, 68 b, 72, 73, 74 a, 114 ; Martin Brigdale pp. 5 bl, 8 al, 14 a, 15, 17 ia, 23, 37 a, 38 al, 45, 46 a, 47 b, 48 al, 52, 53 b, 54 a, 55 br, 57 b, 58 br, 67 l, 76, 88 al, 93 a, 98 cr, 105 ia, 106 l, 116; Peter Cassidy pp. 33 b, 92 r, 104, 105 bk; Jean Cazals pp. 63, 65, 108 br, 112 bl; pp. ; Vanessa Davies p. 43; Laura Edwards pp. 12 bk, 41 bk, 42 bk, 95 bk, 112 bk; Tara Fisher pp. 2 cl, 5 al, 10, 20, 30, 40 a, 50, 60, 70 a, 80, 90 a, 95 ia, 100 ia, 110 l, 120 a; Jonathan Gregson pp. 35, 78 ar, 86, 120, 122 bk, 126 bk; Jeremy Hopley p. 127 l; Richard Jung p. 64, 75, 98 br, 102 l; Sandra Lane p. 97 I. Lisa Linder pp. 42 l, 84 a; William Lingwood pp. 1 ar and bl, 5 br, 11 a, 18 ar, 18 bl, 21 l, 24 l, 25, 26, 27, 31 l, 32 l, 34, 41 l, 44, 51 a, 61 r, 62 l, 71 l, 81 b, 88 br, 91 r, 94, 96 ia, 101 l, 104 l, 107, 108 al, 111 a, 115 ia; Jonathan Lovekin pp. 28 bl, 36, 117 ia; Diana Miller p. 22 r; Steve Painter pp. 2 cr, 16, 56, 85, 99, 100 bk; 103 b. William Reavell p. 12 I; Debi Treloar pp. 77 r, 82 a, 117 bk, 121 b; Ian Wallace p. 113 b; Kate Whitaker pp. 9, 17 bk, 39, 47 bk, 83, 89, 96 bk, 102 bk, 111 bk, 115 bk, 118 br, 119 bk, 122 a, 123 a, 124, 125, 126 l; Polly Wreford pp. 66, 87 r.

Film Photography Credits

All images are courtesy of The Kobal Collection.
20th Century Fox p.1 al, 67 r, 81 a, 91 l; Danjaq/EON/UA pp.1 br, 110 a, 113 a, 115 b, 117 b; Marvel Enterprises pp. 2 al, 101 r, 105 b; Warner Bros./DC Comics p. 2 ar, 98 bl, 106 br; United Artists pp. 2 bl, 32 br, 51 b, 108 bl, 112 br; Jolly/Constantin/Ocean p. 2 br; Castlerock/Nelson/Columbia pp. 5 ac, 28 br, 57 a; Alphaville/IMOHOTEP Prod p. 5 bc, 96 b; ITV Global p. 7; MGM/Pathe p. 8 ar; Dreamworks Pictures pp. 8 lc, 17 b; New Line Cinema/Blankenhorn, Craig p. 8 lc, p. 11; Tri-Star/Osenthal, Zade p. 13 b; MGM/Bennett, Tracy p. 14 b; Zoetrope/Columbia Tri-Star pp. 18 al, 21 r; Orion p. 22 l; Paramount/Bass, Saul pp. 24 l, 18 br, 82 b; Paramount pp. 6, 28 al and ar, 33 ar, 37 b, 68 al, 71 r, Touchstone p. 31 br; Miramax/Universal/Bailey, Alex pp. 38 ar, 42 br; Warner Bros./Mountain, Peter p. 40 b; Polygram/Channel 4/Working Title pp. 38 b, 41 r; Joseph Shaftel Prods p. 46 b; Buena Vista/Touchstone Pictures p. 47 ar; Warner Bros pp. 48 ar and b, 53 a, 55 a, 58 bl, 58 ar, 61 bl, 62 r, 68 ar, 70 b, 74 b; Jolly/Constantin/Ocean pp. 48 c, 54 l; Selznick/MGM p. 58 al; Sony Pictures/Smith, Daniel p. 77 b; Universal p. 78 al, 87 l; Lucasfilm/20Tth Century Fox p. 78 bl, 84 b; Carolco/Tri-Star p. 78 br; Walt Disney pp. 88 bl, 90 b, 95 b; Lawrence Gordon/Mutual Film/Paramount p. 88 ar; NBC-TV p. 92 l; TriStar/Amblin p. 93 b; Marvel Entertainment Group 98 al, 100 b; Columbia/Marvel p. 98 ar; Paramount/Walt Disney Productions p. 102 r; Skydance Productions p. 103 a; Danjaq/ EON Productions p. 108 ar; EON/Danjaq/Sony p. 111 b; EON/Danjaq/UIP p. 114 l; DAMFX pp. 118 a; 127 b; Bend It Films/Film Council pp. 118 b, 123 b; Miraai/Jane Balfour p. 120 b; Red Chillies Ent. p. 121 a; Film 4/Celador Films/Pathe International p. 122 b.

Contents

It's Movie Night

Where do you go when the record is o[...]

Dinner and a movie go together like spaghetti and meatballs, cheese and crackers, Hugh Grant and rom-coms. Having one without the other is perfectly acceptable, but the outcome will lack that certain zing. While a meal and a film are fun activities to be enjoyed out and about, actor Paul Newman said it best when he famously quipped, 'Why go out for a burger when you have steak at home?' He was, of course, talking about his beautiful wife, but the same concept applies here. Why go out to an overpriced restaurant with rude wait staff and a cinema where you run the risk of getting sticky popcorn tangled in your hair when you can enjoy a delicious meal and a great flick in the comfort of your own home?

That's where *Dinner and a Movie* comes in. Each of the 12 chapters outlines a specific film genre and then suggests delectable dishes that you can rustle up to complement the film – or films – you're going to indulge in. So, apart from the food, how else can you make sure your movie night sizzles?

Opening Credits

Before you even think about hitting the kitchen, you can add anticipation to the evening by sending out invitations. You could go for a 'general' film approach using a clapperboard style, or you could tie it in with your specific theme – using the cover of a comic book for a superhero-themed evening, for example.

Set the Scene

Giving your living room the backdrop of a blockbuster will add to the themed fun. If you're planning to screen *Saturday Night Fever*, you could rig up a glitter ball to get the '70s vibe going. Or if *9 to 5* is the film du jour, perhaps set all your clocks to either 9 or 5 o'clock. While people are arriving, you could play the movie's soundtrack. And, if you really want to impress the Joneses next door, you could roll out a red carpet in your driveway, which would be especially apt if you're hosting an Oscars-themed night.

Costume Party

There are countless movies that inspire playing dress-up. If you're screening *Gentlemen Prefer Blondes*, how cool would it be to see your best friend dolled up as Marilyn Monroe while devouring your Sparkling Diamond Cupcakes? Or watching your cousin strut around like John Wayne as he loads up on Texas Whoopie Pies as *True Grit* plays? Give guests plenty of advance warning so they can keep an eye out for clothes and accessories that would fit the bill. You can even award prizes, or extra servings, to those who wow you with their wardrobe.

Get Animated

In the good ol' days, cartoons would always be shown before a movie. Why not bring back this tradition by showing a vintage cartoon like Porky Pig, Woody Woodpecker or Betty Boop before screening your movies? Check out Amazon or eBay and you'll most likely unearth some absolute classics.

Child's Play

If you have kids and are hosting a family movie night, there are plenty of ways to keep them entertained before the film even starts. Have them create a 'box office' that you can keep for future screenings. A large painted cardboard box would be just the ticket. Speaking of tickets, another art project could see the kids designing them for the night, then 'selling' them to you from their box office before the show. They could even play usher and escort you to your seat with a torch like they used to do in cinemas back in the day.

Playing double features is a good way to watch a kid-friendly film first, then a grown-up one after 'intermission', when the kids are tucked up in bed. If you're going for a gangster theme, *Bugsy Malone* followed by *Goodfellas* could be good options.

Question Time

'What year was this movie made?', 'Name three other films this actor appears in?' or 'what's the next line?'. These are just a few questions you can pose to your guests before, during or after the movie you're watching. You can pepper the evening with fun facts that you've previously researched online –IMDb.com is a great resource for film trivia.

Alfresco Flicks

If the weather is going to behave, why not take the party outside? You can buy or hire an inflatable movie screen, and perhaps even hook up some pretty lights for extra ambience. Arrange some comfy chairs and beanbags and soon your garden will resemble a Hollywood haven under the stars.

Hopefully these ideas have given you food for thought, as it were. Themed movie nights hold the potential for enormous creativity and flair – which is what cinematic experiences are all about. Hungry for more? Good. Now, grab your apron and the remote control… it's time for lights, spatula, action!

SUSAN SARANDON   GEENA DAVIS

Somebody said *get a life*...so they did.

A RIDLEY SCOTT FILM

THELMA
&
LOUISE

GIRL POWER

'They say nothing lasts forever; dreams change, trends come and go, but friendships never go out of style.' — *Sex and the City*

Is there anything more wonderfully comforting and entertaining than gathering the girls together for a night of gossip, giggles and gluttony? Either dress up in your most glamorous, fabulous garb or get snug in your comfiest PJs (a onesie isn't out of the question, either) and settle in for a night of fun and flicks. Hair-braiding and pillow fights optional.

Our girlfriends accept us just as we are… wobbly bits and all. We can truly be ourselves around our chicas, which is why the recipes in this chapter say 'fooey' to diets and encourage you to indulge in pure deliciousness. There's no calorie counting, no insecurities and no guilt. Rejoice in the creamy goodness of mac 'n' cheese; melt into the decadent richness of Mississippi mud pie; sink your teeth into a double-decker club sandwich; and delight in the feeling as your silk stocking cocktail slides gloriously down your throat. Tuck in, sister!

IT'S MOVIE NIGHT!

Thelma & Louise, The Color Purple, A League of their Own, 9 to 5, Steel Magnolias, Working Girl, Nancy Drew, The Devil Wears Prada, Bend It Like Beckham, Mulan, Sex and the City, Whip It, Set It Off, Coyote Ugly, Beaches, Little Women, The Sisterhood of the Traveling Pants, Legally Blonde, Matilda, Buffy the Vampire Slayer, Erin Brockovich, The Help, Julie & Julia, The Fabulous Baker Boys, Mean Girls.

BUTTER TOFFEE POPCORN

In the words of Julie Powell in *Julie & Julia*, 'Is there anything better than butter?' Answer: no. Except, perhaps, butter toffee popcorn. The classic accessory to a movie night, popcorn will never disappoint. And butter toffee popcorn will never last longer than the first few scenes.

1–2 tablespoons sunflower or vegetable oil
90 g/⅓ cup popcorn kernels
70 g/5 tablespoons butter
100 g/½ cup light brown sugar
60 ml/¼ cup golden syrup/light corn syrup
1 teaspoon vanilla extract
a pinch of sea salt
Makes 1 large bowl

Heat the oil in a large lidded saucepan with a few popcorn kernels in the pan. When you hear the kernels pop, carefully tip in the rest of the kernels. Shake the pan over the heat until the popping stops. Take care when lifting the lid as any unpopped kernels may still pop from the heat of the pan. Tip the popcorn into a bowl, removing any unpopped kernels as you go. Put the butter, sugar, syrup, vanilla extract and salt in a small saucepan and simmer gently, stirring frequently, until the butter has melted and the sugar has dissolved. You should be left with a thick toffee sauce. Pour the warm toffee sauce over the popcorn, stirring well so that the popcorn is evenly coated. Serve either warm or cold, but if eating cold, make sure that you stir the popcorn every 20 minutes or so as it cools to prevent it sticking together.

SILK STOCKING

What would the *Sex and the City* foursome be without their regular fix of cocktails? Not nearly as entertaining, most likely! The luscious crème de cacao and cream that go into this bevvy of beauty invite you to sink further into the sofa as you take a long sip and smile contentedly.

35 ml/1¼ oz. tequila
15 ml/½ oz. white crème de cacao
1 barspoon grenadine
15 ml/½ oz. double/ heavy cream
2 fresh raspberries, to garnish
Serves 1

Add all the ingredients to a blender. Add two scoops of crushed ice and blend for 20 seconds. Pour the mixture into a hurricane glass, garnish with the raspberries and serve with 2 straws.

MEAN GIRLS' MUFFINS

While 'Is your muffin buttered?' is a ridiculous and crude question posed by a silly boy in *Mean Girls*, these yummy treats would actually be rather delicious with a little butter spread on when serving. And if they're straight out of the oven, so much the tastier.

200 g/1½ cups self-raising/self-rising wholemeal/whole wheat flour
1 tablespoon baking powder
½ teaspoon sea salt
100 g/⅔ cup polenta or cornmeal
1 teaspoon cumin seeds
½–1 red chilli/chile, deseeded and finely chopped

2 tablespoons chopped fresh coriander/cilantro
60 g/½ cup fresh or frozen sweetcorn kernels
300 ml/1¼ cups milk
1 egg, beaten
3 tablespoons sunflower oil
freshly ground black pepper
12-hole nonstick muffin pan, lightly greased
Makes 12

Sift the flour, baking powder and salt into a mixing bowl, tipping in any bran left in the sieve/strainer. Add a grinding of black pepper, then stir in the polenta, cumin seeds, chilli/chile, coriander/cilantro and sweetcorn kernels. Mix the milk, egg and sunflower oil together, then pour into the dry ingredients and stir together briefly until just mixed. Spoon into the prepared muffin pan, then bake in a preheated oven at 190°C (375°F) Gas 5 for 20 minutes until risen, firm and lightly browned. Remove the muffins from the pan and let cool on a wire rack before serving.

FIESTY FRIED CHICKEN

Fried chicken is widely believed to have originated in the American South. You know what film stars six spicy chicks and was set in the American South? *Steel Magnolias*. With just the right amount of kick, these chicken pieces will accompany you through the lives, loves, losses and laughs of these Louisiana ladies.

3 boneless, skinless chicken breasts
150 ml/⅔ cup buttermilk
100 g/¾ cup plain/all-purpose flour
1 generous teaspoon baking powder
1 generous teaspoon sea salt flakes
½ teaspoon ground cayenne pepper
½ teaspoon Spanish smoked paprika
¼ teaspoon ground coriander
¼ teaspoon garlic powder
a pinch of ground allspice
½ teaspoon dried oregano
freshly ground black pepper
sunflower oil, for frying
Serves 4

Cut each chicken breast into 5 or 6 strips. Place in a ceramic dish and coat with the buttermilk. Cover with clingfilm/plastic wrap and chill for at least 2 hours. Remove the chicken from the buttermilk and pat off any excess with kitchen paper/paper towels. Combine the flour, baking powder, salt flakes, spices, oregano and some black pepper in a bowl. Toss the chicken pieces in the seasoned flour and set aside on nonstick parchment paper for 10 minutes. Pour 3–4 tablespoons sunflower oil in a frying pan. Set over medium heat and add one-third of the chicken pieces. Cook until golden and crispy. Drain on kitchen paper/paper towels and repeat with the remaining 2 batches of chicken.

HIT THE CLUB SANDWICH

Get your chops around this double-decker bacon and turkey club sandwich. Eating it may not be ladylike but who cares, it's not like there are any guys around to impress tonight. Chomp!

12 slices of thick white bread
4 tablespoons mayonnaise
8 slices of deli turkey
4 crisp leaves of butter lettuce
1 avocado, pitted, peeled and
   thinly sliced

8 paper-thin red onion slices
8 grilled, crispy dry-cured
   bacon slices
4 slices of beefsteak tomato
cocktail sticks/toothpicks
Serves 4

Toast the bread, then spread one side of each piece of toast with the mayonnaise. Stack the turkey, lettuce and avocado on 4 of these and top with another piece of toast. Stack the red onion, bacon and tomato over and top with the remaining toast. Cut the sandwich in half diagonally and then again diagonally in the opposite direction. Secure all 4 pieces with a cocktail stick/toothpick. Repeat with the other 3 sandwiches. Serve with potato salad.

DREAMY MAC 'N' CHEESE

Carbs? Check. Cheese? Check. Feeling of complete and utter satisfaction?
Check. This dreamy, creamy dish will make you and your girls feel all warm
and fuzzy inside – which is what 'Girl Power' movie night is all about.

**60 g/1⅓ cup fresh,
   chunky breadcrumbs**
1 tablespoon olive oil
25 g/2 tablespoons butter
**1 garlic clove, finely
   chopped**
1 teaspoon dry mustard
**3 tablespoons plain/
   all-purpose flour**
500 ml/2 cups milk
**125 ml/½ cup
   mascarpone**
**130 g/1¼ cups grated
   mature/sharp Cheddar
   cheese**
**60 g/½ cup grated
   Parmesan cheese**
**350 g/12 oz. rigatoni or
   macaroni**
**sea salt and freshly
   ground black pepper**
21 x 21 cm/8 x 8 inch
baking dish

Serves 4

Preheat the oven to 200°C (400°F) Gas 6. Spread the breadcrumbs on a baking
sheet, drizzle with the oil and season. Bake for 6 minutes, remove and set aside.
Melt the butter in a medium saucepan. Add the garlic and mustard and sauté
for 1 minute before adding the flour. Whisk constantly over medium heat until
it forms a paste. Gradually whisk in the milk and turn up the heat. Bring to the
boil, whisking constantly. Turn the heat down to low and simmer for 10
minutes. Remove from the heat and add the mascarpone, Cheddar and half of
the Parmesan. Boil the pasta in salted water until just al dente, drain and mix
with the cheese sauce. Season and spoon the mixture into the baking dish. Top
with the breadcrumbs and the remaining Parmesan. Bake for 20 minutes until
golden. Let sit for 5 minutes before serving.

125 g/1 stick unsalted
   butter, softened
1 tablespoon smooth
   peanut butter
200 g/1 cup (caster) sugar
1 large egg
320 g/2⅓ cups self-
   raising/self-rising flour
1 teaspoon baking
   powder
½ teaspoon salt
250 ml/1 cup buttermilk
100 ml/⅓ cup hot water
Peanut glaze
15 g/1 tablespoon butter
1 tablespoon smooth
   peanut butter
150 g/1¼ cups icing/
   confectioners' sugar
50 g/⅓ cup salted
   peanuts, chopped
Filling
70 g/5 tablespoons
   butter, softened
2 tablespoons smooth
   peanut butter
200 g/1⅔ cups icing/
   confectioners' sugar
3 tablespoons sour cream
3 tablespoons raspberry
   jam
two 12-hole whoopie
pie pans, greased
piping bag with a large
star nozzle/tip (optional)
Makes 12

MAKIN' WHOOPEE PIES

Nominated for an Oscar as Best Actress in a Leading Role for her performance in *The Fabulous Baker Boys*, Michelle Pfeiffer writhes around on a piano while singing Makin' Whoopee. Why not imagine you're just as seductive as you whip up some whoopee of your own?

Preheat the oven to 180°C (350°F) Gas 4. To make the pies, cream together the butter, peanut butter and sugar in a mixing bowl for 2–3 minutes using an electric hand-held mixer until light and creamy. Add the egg and mix again. Sift the flour and baking powder into the bowl and add the salt and buttermilk. Whisk again until everything is incorporated. Add the hot water and whisk into the mixture. Put a large spoonful of mixture into each hole in the prepared pans. Let stand

for 10 minutes, then bake each pan in the preheated oven for 10–12 minutes. Remove the pies from the oven, let cool slightly then turn out onto a wire rack. To make the peanut glaze, heat the butter, peanut butter, icing/confectioners' sugar and 60 ml/¼ cup cold water in a saucepan set over low heat. Simmer until you have a smooth, thick glaze, then spoon this over half of the pie halves. Let cool completely. To make the filling, whisk together the butter, peanut butter, icing/confectioners' sugar and sour cream in a mixing bowl using an electric hand-held mixer, until light and creamy. Spoon the filling into the prepared piping bag and pipe stars of filling in a ring onto the 12 unglazed pie halves – reserving a little to decorate. (If you do not have a piping bag, thickly spread the filling over the pie halves with a round-bladed knife.) Put a spoonful of jam on top of the filling and top with the glazed pie halves. Pipe a star of the reserved filling on top of each one, sprinkle with the chopped peanuts and serve.

MISSISSIPPI MMM PIE

Set in the US state of Mississippi, *The Help* would be the perfect film to accompany this delectable dessert. Just make sure you finish eating it before you get to the scene where Minny serves a chocolate pie.

Biscuit base
225 g/8 oz. digestive biscuits/graham crackers
60 g/2 oz. dark/semisweet chocolate
50 g/4 tablespoons butter
Chocolate filling
180 g/6 oz. dark/semisweet chocolate
180 g/1½ sticks butter, chopped
4 large eggs, beaten
90 g/½ cup light brown sugar
90 g/½ cup dark brown sugar
180 ml/¾ cup double/heavy cream
Chocolate cream
140 ml/⅔ cup double/heavy cream, chilled
3 tablespoons cocoa powder
40 g/⅓ cup icing/confectioners' sugar
23-cm/9-inch springform cake pan, greased

Serves 8

To make the base, put the biscuits/crackers into a food processor and process until fine crumbs form. Chop the chocolate and put it in a heatproof bowl set over a saucepan of steaming but not boiling water and melt gently with the butter (do not let the base of the bowl touch the water). Remove from the heat, stir gently, then stir into the biscuit/cracker crumbs. When well mixed, transfer the mixture to the prepared pan and, using the back of a spoon, press onto the base and about halfway up the sides of the tin. Chill while making the filling. To make the filling, chop the chocolate, put it in a heatproof bowl set over a saucepan of steaming but not boiling water and melt gently with the butter (do not let the base of the bowl touch the water). Remove from the heat, stir gently, then let cool. Put the eggs and sugars into a large mixing bowl and, using an electric hand-held whisk or mixer, whisk until thick and foamy. Whisk in the cream followed by the melted chocolate mixture. Pour the mixture onto the base and bake in a preheated oven at 180°C (350°F) Gas 4 for about 45 minutes until just firm. Let cool for a few minutes, then remove from the pan. To make the chocolate cream, put the cream into a mixing bowl, then sift the cocoa and icing/confectioners' sugar on top and stir gently with a wooden spoon until blended. Cover and chill for 2 hours. Serve the pie with the chocolate cream.

LOVE
NEVER
DIES

BRAM STOKER'S
Dracula

A FRANCIS FORD COPPOLA FILM
COLUMBIA PICTURES

A new-
and altogether
different—
screen
excitement!!!

Starring
ANTHONY
PERKINS

VERA
MILES

JOHN
GAVIN

co-starring
MARTIN
BALSAM

JOHN
McINTIRE

and
JANET
LEIGH
as MARION
CRANE

ALFRED
HITCHCOCK'S

PSYCHO

Directed by
ALFRED
HITCHCOCK

Screenplay by
JOSEPH
STEFANO

A PARAMOUNT
Release

FRIGHT NIGHT

'I ATE HIS LIVER WITH SOME FAVA BEANS AND A NICE CHIANTI' – *The Silence of the Lambs*

Do you have the guts to host a petrifying movie night that scares your guests silly? Mwah ha ha! As well as preparing a killer spread – think coffin sandwiches, meringue bones and graveyard cupcakes – you could get the eerie atmosphere going with fake cobwebs, spiders, bugs and skeletons adorning your living room. And if your guests think they can escape the fear by going to the bathroom, they've got another thing coming... buy a *Psycho* shower curtain and 'bloody' bathmat to unnerve them even more. Make sure the lights are dimmed throughout the night so as not to break the spooky spell. If you want your companions to really jump out of their skin, you could always enlist the help of a friend who's not at the movie night to bang on your window at a particularly tense moment during the film. Eek!

IT'S MOVIE NIGHT!

28 Days Later, Hellraiser, Dracula, Carrie, Jaws, The Shining, Let the Right One In, The Silence of the Lambs, The Exorcist, The Others, Re-Animator, The Sixth Sense, Eraserhead, The Haunting, Halloween, Ghostbusters, Friday the 13th, The Addams Family, Psycho, Scream, Pet Sematary, Night of the Living Dead, Shaun of the Dead, It, Children of the Corn.

PARANOIA POPCORN

1–2 tablespoons sunflower or vegetable oil
90 g/⅓ cup mini popcorn kernels
sea salt and freshly ground black pepper
Makes 1 large bowl

Simple and moreish, gobble this snack while watching *Arachnophobia*. Just be sure to check each mouthful — you don't want to meet the same horrific fate as popcorn-munching Irv and Blaire.

Heat the oil in a large lidded saucepan with a few popcorn kernels in the pan. When you hear the kernels pop, carefully tip in the rest of the kernels. Shake the pan over the heat until the popping stops. Take care when lifting the lid, as any unpopped kernels may still pop from the heat of the pan. Tip the popcorn into a bowl, removing any unpopped kernels as you go. Season the popcorn well with salt and pepper and serve warm or cold.

BLOODY MARY

There's Something About Mary... She's bleeding all over the place! Or is that one of *Dracula's* victims? This cocktail with a kick is the ideal drink to serve on Fright Night – what other beverage would be suitably fiery when dining with the devil?

50 ml/1¾ oz. vodka
300 ml/1¼ cups tomato juice
pinch of ground black pepper
2 dashes of Worcestershire sauce
2 dashes of Tabasco sauce
2 dashes of lemon juice
barspoon horseradish sauce
celery stalk, to garnish
Serves 1

LOVE
NEVER
DIES

BRAM STOKER'S
Dracula

A FRANCIS FORD COPPOLA FILM
COLUMBIA PICTURES PRESENTS

OSIRIS FILMS PRODUCTION "BRAM STOKER'S DRACULA" GARY OLDMAN WINONA RYDER ANTHONY HOPKINS KEANU REEVES
JAMES V. HART ROMAN COPPOLA MUSIC WOJCIECH KILAR COSTUME DESIGNER EIKO ISHIOKA EDITED NICHOLAS C. SMITH GLEN SCANTLEBURY ANNE GOURSAUD
DESIGNER THOMAS SANDERS DIRECTOR MICHAEL BALLHAUS, A.S.C. EXECUTIVE MICHAEL APTED AND ROBERT O'CONNOR SCREENPLAY JAMES V. HART
PRODUCED FRANCIS FORD COPPOLA, FRED FUCHS AND CHARLES MULVEHILL DIRECTED FRANCIS FORD COPPOLA

FROM
AMERICAN ZOETROPE

COLUMBIA
PICTURES

Shake all the ingredients over ice and strain into a highball filled with ice. Garnish with a celery stalk. To make a Bloody Shame, simply leave out the vodka.

MURDEROUSLY MARINATED BEEF SUSHI

Rice wrapped in flesh is the perfect morsel to feed your
victims... sorry, guests. The taste is intense and intoxicating
- once it has a hold of you, it won't let you go.

2 teaspoons groundnut/peanut oil
300 g/10½ oz. beef eye fillet, in one piece
2 tablespoons Japanese soy sauce
2 tablespoons mirin (sweetened Japanese rice wine)
2 tablespoons rice vinegar
500g/2½ cups cooked sushi rice
shredded pickled cabbage and ginger, to serve

Serves 4–6

To prepare the beef, heat the oil in a frying pan and
sear the beef on all sides until browned. Mix the soy
sauce, mirin and vinegar in a bowl and pour over
the beef, turning the beef to coat. Remove from the
heat and transfer the beef and its sauce to a dish. Let
cool, cover and refrigerate for 1 hour, turning once.
Divide the rice into 18 balls, the size of a walnut and
shape into firm ovals. Cut the beef in half lengthways
(along the natural separation line), then slice as
finely as possible. Wrap a piece of beef around the
top of a rice ball and top with a little pickled
cabbage or ginger.

GOTHIC RISOTTO

600 g/1¼ lbs. cleaned squid plus 2 sachets/envelopes squid ink
3 tablespoons extra virgin olive oil
½ onion, finely chopped
1 garlic clove, finely chopped
about 1.5 litres/6 cups hot fish stock
150 ml/⅔ cup dry white wine
500 g/2½ cups risotto rice
50 g/4 tablespoons unsalted butter, softened
2 tablespoons grappa (optional)
3 tablespoons finely chopped fresh flat-leaf parsley
sea salt and freshly ground black pepper
freshly grated Parmesan cheese, to serve (optional)

Serves 4–6

Surely a much-loved and much-scoffed meal around *The Addams Family* dinner table, this deathly dish will take you to the dark side and unleash your inner demon.

To prepare squid, rinse it, then pull the tentacles and head away from the body. Carefully remove the silvery ink sacs from the heads without piercing them. Cut off all the internal organs still attached to the head. Put the ink sacs in a tea strainer over a small bowl and press out the ink with the back of a spoon. Cut the squid body and tentacles into thin rings and small pieces. Keep some of the tentacles whole if you like. Heat the oil in a saucepan and add the onion and garlic. Cook gently for 10 minutes until soft, golden and translucent but not browned. Add the squid, 2 ladles of the stock and the wine, then cover and cook gently for about 20 minutes or until tender, adding a little stock to the pan if necessary during cooking. Add the rice and stir until well coated with the squid mixture and heated through. Mix the ink with a little stock and stir into the risotto. Begin adding the stock, a large ladle at a time, stirring gently until each ladle has almost been absorbed by the rice. The risotto should be kept at a bare simmer throughout cooking – add more stock as necessary. Continue until the rice is tender and creamy but the grains are still firm. This should take 15–20 minutes depending on the type of rice used. Taste and season well with salt and pepper and beat in the butter and grappa (if using). Cover and let rest for a couple of minutes, then serve immediately topped with the chopped parsley, together with a bowl of Parmesan, if liked.

MERINGUE BONES

200 g/1 cup (caster) sugar
100 g/3½ oz. egg whites
(from 3–4 eggs)
a pinch of salt
2 solid baking sheets lined
with nonstick parchment
paper
piping bag with a plain
1-cm/⅜-inch nozzle/tip
Makes about 20

These meringue bones
will inspire you to
relive the ultimate
'eek' moment when
Norman Bates's
skeletal mother is
revealed in *Psycho*.
That is, if you
haven't lost
your appetite.

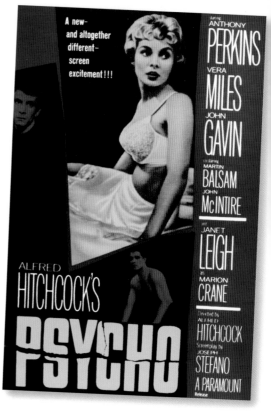

Preheat the oven to 200°C
(400°F) Gas 6. Tip the
sugar into a small roasting
pan and place on the
middle shelf of the
preheated oven for about
4 minutes or until hot to
the touch. When the sugar is hot enough, turn the oven down to 110°C (225°F)
Gas ¼. Whisk the egg whites with a pinch of salt in the bowl of a free-standing
electric mixer until foamy. Quickly tip all of the hot sugar into the bowl and
whisk on medium-high speed for about 6 minutes until the meringue is very
thick, glossy and white. Spoon the meringue into the piping bag. Pipe 10 log
shapes, each about 10 cm/4 inches long, on each prepared baking sheet,
spacing them well apart. Pipe 2 balls of meringue at each end of the logs to
make a bone shape. Bake on the middle shelf of the oven for about 40 minutes
or until crisp. Turn the oven off and leave the bones inside until cold.

COFFIN SANDWICHES

These eerie sarnies will breathe some afterlife into your party. Zombie films like *Night of the Living Dead* or *Shaun of the Dead* will complement this RIP recipe perfectly. Watch as guests creak them open, trying to discover if what's inside is safe to eat.

Cinnamon cookie dough
225 g/2 sticks unsalted butter, softened
225 g/1 cup plus 2 tablespoons (caster) sugar
finely grated zest of ½ orange
1 large egg, lightly beaten
½ teaspoon ground cinnamon
a pinch of salt
450 g/3⅔ cups plain/all-purpose flour

Filling
100 g/3½ oz. dark/semisweet chocolate, chopped
100 g/⅓ cup sweetened condensed milk
40 g/3 tablespoons unsalted butter, softened
To decorate
100 g/3½oz. dark/semisweet chocolate, chopped
100 g/3½ oz. white chocolate, chopped
baking sheets, lined with nonstick parchment paper
piping bag with a fine, round nozzle/tip
Makes 8–10

Put the butter and sugar in a mixing bowl and cream until pale and light. Add the orange zest, egg, cinnamon and salt and mix. Add the flour and mix until incorporated. Bring the dough together into a ball, wrap in clingfilm/plastic wrap and chill for 2 hours. Preheat the oven to 180°C (350°F) Gas 4. Roll out the dough to a thickness of 2–3 mm/⅛ inch. Cut out as many rectangles as possible, 12 cm/5 inches long and 6 cm/2½ inches wide. Stack 4 rectangles on top of each other and trim triangles off the corners to make coffin shapes. Repeat. Arrange on the baking sheets. Bake for 12 minutes. Let cool on the baking sheets for 10 minutes, then on a wire rack until cold. To make the filling, tip all the ingredients into a heatproof bowl and melt over a saucepan of barely simmering water. Stir until smooth, then spread the filling over half of the cookies and top with another coffin. To decorate, melt the dark and white chocolates in separate bowls and stir until smooth. Spoon half of the dark chocolate into the white chocolate and stir to swirl. Brush the top of each coffin with the marbled chocolate and let set. Fill the piping bag with the remaining dark chocolate and pipe a border and initials on the top of each coffin.

SEVERED FINGERS

Pointedly horrific, you could either serve up these monster munchies on their own so your movie viewers know what they're about to sink their teeth into, or you could hide them in the other dishes you're serving as a sinister surprise. Either way, this is one party where your guests will most definitely be getting digits.

125 g/1 stick unsalted
   butter, softened
25 g/2 tablespoons
   (caster) sugar
100 g/¾ cup icing/
   confectioners' sugar
2 large egg yolks
1 teaspoon pure vanilla
   extract
275 g/2 cups plus 2
   tablespoons plain/
   all-purpose flour
½ teaspoon baking
   powder
a pinch of salt
20 whole almonds,
   halved (allowing extra
   for breakages)
baking sheet, lined with
nonstick parchment paper
Makes about 24

Preheat the oven to 180°C (350°F) Gas 4. Put the butter, and sugars in a mixing bowl and cream until pale and light. Add the egg yolks and vanilla extract and mix until combined. Add the flour, baking powder and salt and mix again until smooth. Break off small balls of dough and roll between your hands to make sausage shapes. Roll them no thicker than your own fingers. A good way to get a realistic finger effect is to splay your fingers when you roll your hand over the sausage of dough – you should get a bumpy outline to represent knuckles. Arrange on the prepared baking sheet. Press half an almond, flat side up, onto the end of each finger as a fingernail and use a round-bladed knife to mark ridges on each knuckle bone. Bake in batches on the middle shelf of the preheated oven for about 12 minutes until pale golden and firm. Let cool on the baking sheet for 2–3 minutes before transferring to a wire rack until cold. Serve in individual boxes for an extra spooky surprise!

GRAVEYARD CUPCAKES

You've heard of death by chocolate, how about death by cupcake? *Pet Sematary* would be a suitably spooky film to watch while nibbling on these disturbingly delicious burial-ground bites.

Cupcakes

175 g/1½ sticks unsalted butter, softened

250 g/1¼ cups (caster) sugar

2 large eggs, beaten

1 teaspoon vanilla extract

½ teaspoon red food colouring

125 ml/½ cup buttermilk, at room temperature

175 g/1⅓ cups plain/all-purpose flour

2 tablespoons unsweetened cocoa powder

a pinch of salt

1 teaspoon bicarbonate of soda/baking soda

1 teaspoon white vinegar

To decorate

½ quantity cinnamon cookie dough from Coffin Sandwiches (page 25)

150 g/1¼ cups royal icing/confectioners' sugar

black food colouring

450 g/1 lb. ready-made chocolate frosting

6 Oreo cookies, crushed

sugarpaste or marzipan pumpkins, to decorate

12-hole muffin pan, lined with 12 black or brown cupcake cases

2 baking sheets, lined with nonstick parchment paper

Makes 12

Preheat the oven to 180°C (350°F) Gas 4. To make the cupcakes, cream the butter and sugar together until pale and light. Gradually add the eggs and vanilla and mix well. Mix the red food colouring with the buttermilk in a separate bowl. In another bowl, sift together the flour, cocoa and salt. Add the dry ingredients in alternate batches with the red buttermilk and mix until smooth. Mix together the bicarbonate of soda/baking soda and vinegar and mix into the cake batter. Divide the mixture between the cake cases and bake in the oven for about 20 minutes until well risen. For the gravestones, roll out the cookie dough on a clean, lightly floured work surface and cut out 12 crosses. Arrange on the baking sheets and bake in the oven for 10–12 minutes until golden. Cool on the baking sheets. Mix the royal icing/confectioners' sugar with enough water to make a thick icing and tint it black using the food colouring. Spoon the icing into a piping bag and pipe an outline onto each headstone. Cover the top of each cupcake with chocolate frosting, scatter over the crushed cookies and push the headstone into one side. Decorate with the pumpkins and serve.

AUDREY
HEPBURN

PLAYS THAT DARING, DARLING
HOLLY GOLIGHTLY TO A NEW HIGH
IN ENTERTAINMENT DELIGHT!

BREAKFAST
AT TIFFANY'S

GEORGE PEPPARD · NEAL · EBSEN · BALSAM AND MICKEY ROONEY

TECHNICOLOR

The Big Apple

'The place: New York City. The time: Now, 1962. And there's no time or place like it. If you've got a dream, this is the place to make that dream come true.'
— *Down with Love*

New York City is, basically, one giant film set. It's been described as one of the most cinematic cities in the world, so you don't have to have actually been there to know and love it. From the yellow cabs to Rockefeller Center, Central Park to the Brooklyn Bridge, everything is familiar because you'll have visited this bustling city countless times via the movies. For your New York-themed film night, let your imagination run wild. Buy a big blackboard and draw the NYC skyline on there, including landmarks like the Statue of Liberty, the Empire State Building and the Chrysler Building (geographical accuracy isn't important!); set the dinner table up with placemats and coasters with New York scenes on; provide napkins with the subway map printed on; and give guests stickers that declare 'I heart NY'.

IT'S SHOWTIME!

Sleepless In Seattle, When Harry Met Sally, Taxi Driver, Big, Manhattan, King Kong, Wall Street, Annie Hall, Saturday Night Fever, Down with Love, Gangs of New York, Home Alone 2: Lost in New York, Breakfast at Tiffany's, West Side Story, Shaft, Desperately Seeking Susan, Kids, Stuart Little, Man on Wire, American Psycho, Coming to America, Week-End at the Waldorf, Maid in Manhattan, Cocktail, Look Who's Talking Too.

Raspberry & White Chocolate Popcorn

If you're planning to watch *Look Who's Talking Too*, run a sweepstake before you start the film asking at what exact time Mikey starts yelling, 'Popcorn! Popcorn!' After this scene plays, serve this delicious snack – the winner receiving the biggest portion.

1–2 tablespoons sunflower or vegetable oil
90 g/⅓ cup popcorn kernels
100 g/7 tablespoons butter
1 teaspoon vanilla extract

15 g/2 tablespoons freeze-dried raspberry powder
100 g/½ cup white chocolate chips

Makes 1 large bowl

Heat the oil in a large lidded saucepan with a few popcorn kernels in the pan. When you hear the kernels pop, carefully tip in the rest of the kernels. Shake the pan over the heat until the popping stops. Take care when lifting the lid, as any unpopped kernels may pop from the heat of the pan. Tip the popcorn into a bowl, removing any unpopped kernels as you go. Melt the butter in a small saucepan and add the vanilla extract. Pour the butter over the popcorn and stir well so that it evenly coats the popcorn. Sprinkle over the raspberry powder and stir in the white chocolate chips while the popcorn is still warm so that the chocolate melts into the popcorn. This popcorn can be eaten warm or cold.

Manhattan

How many drinks do you think Tom Cruise served during his stint as a bottle-flinging, fast-pouring Manhattan bartender in *Cocktail*? A fair few, that's for sure. Your guests will get a kick out of sipping this classy drink while drinking in Tom's mischievous performance.

50 ml/1¾ oz. rye whiskey
10 ml/2 barspoons sweet vermouth
10 ml/2 barspoons dry vermouth
2 dashes of Angostura bitters
1 strip orange zest, to garnish
Serves 1

Add the ingredients to a mixing glass filled with ice (first ensure all the ingredients are very cold) and stir the mixture until chilled. Strain into a chilled cocktail glass, add the garnish and serve.

Long Island Iced Tea

Arguably Woody Allen's finest film, many scenes from *Annie Hall* were filmed on Long Island – including the famous lobster scene. After your guests have consumed a couple of these potent cocktails, their love for New York will undoubtedly flow more freely around the room.

30 ml/1 oz. vodka
30 ml/1 oz. gin
30 ml/1 oz. white rum
30 ml/1 oz. tequila
30 ml/1 oz. triple sec
20 ml/¾ oz. freshly squeezed lemon juice
cola, to top up
lemon slices, to serve
Serves 1

Fill a cocktail shaker with ice and add all of the ingredients except the cola. Shake briskly, then pour into a tall glass. Top up with a splash of cola and add a few lemon slices and some more ice, if liked. Serve immediately.

ANNIE HALL
WINS 4 MAJOR ACADEMY AWARDS
BEST PICTURE
BEST ACTRESS BEST DIRECTOR
DIANE KEATON WOODY ALLEN
BEST ORIGINAL SCREENPLAY
WOODY ALLEN AND MARSHALL BRICKMAN

WOODY DIANE TONY CAROL PAUL JANET SHELLEY CHRISTOPHER COLLEEN
ALLEN KEATON ROBERTS KANE SIMON MARGOLIN DUVALL WALKEN DEWHURST

"ANNIE HALL"
A JACK ROLLINS-CHARLES H. JOFFE PRODUCTION
Written by WOODY ALLEN and MARSHALL BRICKMAN · Directed by WOODY ALLEN
Produced by CHARLES H. JOFFE
United Artists

Waldorf Salad

What better way to take a bite out of The Big Apple than to, er, take a bite out of a big apple? This crunch-tastic salad was first created at the Waldorf Hotel (now the Waldorf-Astoria Hotel) in New York, which later became a location for over 20 films, including *Coming to America* and *Week-End at the Waldorf*.

3–4 Granny Smith apples
juice of 1 lemon
2 celery stalks, thinly sliced
125 g/1 cup coarsely chopped walnut
    pieces or pecans
125 ml/½ cup mayonnaise
Serves 4

To prepare the salad, cut a few slices of apple with skin for decoration, then peel and core the remainder and cut into matchstick strips, using a mandoline. Toss them in the lemon juice to stop them turning brown. Finely slice the celery, put into a bowl, add the apples and walnuts, then spoon over the mayonnaise.

New York Deli Bagels With Lox & Cream Cheese

2 bagels

100 g/½ cup cream cheese

125 g/4½ oz. slices of smoked salmon/lox

lemon wedges

freshly ground black pepper

Serves 2

Bagels with lox – a type of smoked salmon – were previously only found in New York delis. It's been said that bagels were once given to women during childbirth and that they symbolized the circle of life, while the lox represented the saltiness of tears. Deep stuff.

Split the bagels in half horizontally and toast on both sides in a toaster, under the grill/broiler or using a stove-top griddle/grill pan. Spread the bottom half of each bagel with cream cheese and fold the slices of smoked salmon/lox on top. Squeeze over plenty of lemon juice, sprinkle with black pepper and serve topped with the second half of the bagel.

Rollin' Reuben

It's been alleged that the Reuben sandwich was created in New York. There are often variations on this traditional fare, but here it'll be served with beef, sauerkraut and emmental cheese. Yum!

4 tablespoons mayonnaise
3 spring onions/scallions, sliced
2 gherkins/pickles, chopped
¼ teaspoon hot horseradish sauce
a dash of Worcestershire sauce
a pinch of sugar
8 slices of rye bread
300 g/10½ oz. salt beef, sliced
200 g/1⅓ cups sauerkraut, drained
100 g/3½ oz. Emmental, sliced
Serves 4

Put the mayonnaise, spring onions/ scallions, gherkins/pickles, horseradish and Worcestershire sauces and sugar in a bowl, mix well and set aside. Preheat the grill/broiler. Grill/broil the bread for 1–2 minutes on one side until golden. Remove from the oven and spread dressing over the untoasted side of half the slices. Lay the Emmental on the rest and grill/broil for 2–3 minutes to melt. Meanwhile, put the beef, then the sauerkraut over the mayonnaise-covered bread slices. Once the cheese has melted, make up the sandwiches and serve immediately.

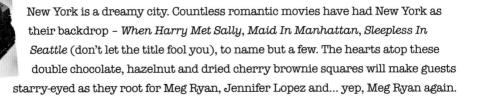

I ♥ NY Chocolate Brownies

New York is a dreamy city. Countless romantic movies have had New York as their backdrop – *When Harry Met Sally, Maid In Manhattan, Sleepless In Seattle* (don't let the title fool you), to name but a few. The hearts atop these double chocolate, hazelnut and dried cherry brownie squares will make guests starry-eyed as they root for Meg Ryan, Jennifer Lopez and... yep, Meg Ryan again.

150 g/1 cup skinned hazelnuts
225 g/8 oz. dark/semisweet chocolate, chopped
150 g/1⅓ sticks unsalted butter
4 eggs
300 g/1½ cups light brown sugar
1 teaspoon vanilla extract
125 g/1 cup plain/all-purpose flour
125 g/scant 1 cup dried cherries
Chocolate fudge frosting
175 g/6 oz. dark/semisweet chocolate, chopped
125 g/1 stick unsalted butter
115 ml/scant ½ cup milk
½ teaspoon vanilla extract
225 g/2 cups icing/confectioners' sugar, sifted
Chocolate hearts
150 g/5½ oz. dark/semisweet chocolate, chopped
pink and/or red sprinkles
23-cm/9-inch square baking pan, lined with nonstick parchment paper
assorted heart-shaped cutters, oiled
2 solid baking sheets, 1 lined with nonstick parchment paper

Makes about 16

Preheat the oven to 180°C (350°F) Gas 4. Put the hazelnuts on a baking sheet and toast in the oven for 5 minutes. Let cool slightly, then chop and set aside. Leave the oven on. Put the chocolate and butter in a heatproof bowl set over a pan of barely simmering water. Stir until smooth and thoroughly combined. Let cool slightly. Put the eggs and sugar in a free-standing electric mixer fitted with the whisk attachment and beat until pale and light. Add the vanilla and chocolate mixture and mix until combined. Sift the flour and fold into the mixture with the chopped hazelnuts and cherries. Pour the mixture into the prepared baking pan and bake on the middle shelf of the hot oven for 25 minutes. Let cool in the pan until completely cold. To make the chocolate fudge frosting, put the chocolate and butter in a heatproof bowl set over a pan of simmering water. Stir until smooth and combined. Set aside to cool slightly. In another bowl, whisk together the milk, vanilla and icing/confectioners' sugar until smooth. Add the cooled chocolate mixture and stir until smooth. Spread the frosting over the brownie and let set before cutting into squares. To make the chocolate hearts, melt the chocolate in a heatproof bowl set over a pan of barely simmering water. Pour the melted chocolate onto the prepared baking sheet and spread into a thin layer using a palette knife. Scatter with pink and/or red sprinkles and let set. Cut out hearts using the heart-shaped cutters. Put the hearts on top of the brownies just before serving.

New York Cheesecake

Rich and smooth, just like Christian Bale in *American Psycho* (you know, before he goes nutty while naked with a chainsaw), New York cheesecake will be a sweet treat to counterbalance the shock of watching this handsome devil losing his marbles.

200 g/7 oz. chocolate
   digestive biscuits/graham
   crackers
60 g/4½ tablespoons butter
1 kg/2¼ lbs. cream cheese
250 g/1¼ cups (caster) sugar
grated zest and freshly
   squeezed juice of 1 lemon
200 ml/1 cup sour cream

2 tablespoons vanilla extract
5 eggs
4 tablespoons plain/
   all-purpose flour
a handful of mixed berries

a 20-cm/8-inch round
springform cake pan
Serves 8–10

Preheat the oven to 140°C (275°F) Gas 1. Crush the biscuits/crackers in a food processor. Melt the butter and add to the crushed biscuits/crackers. Mix well. Press the mixture firmly into the cake pan. Bake for 5 minutes, remove and let cool. Grease the sides of the pan above the crust. In a large bowl, beat the cream cheese and sugar with an electric whisk. Add the lemon zest and juice, sour cream and vanilla extract. Mix until smooth and add the eggs one at a time until well combined. Put the flour in last and mix again. Pour the mixture into the cake pan. Bake for 70 minutes until it is firm and the top is turning light golden. Let sit in the oven with the door open until cool (about 2 hours), then refrigerate for at least 6 hours or overnight. Put the berries on top and serve.

BEST OF BRITISH

'Would you like something to eat? Something to nibble? Apricots soaked in honey? Quite why, no one knows, because it stops them tasting like apricots and makes them taste like honey… and if you wanted honey, you could just… buy honey. Instead of apricots. But, nevertheless, they're yours if you want them.' — *Notting Hill*

Give your guests the royal treatment with a British-themed movie night. Whether you go down the 'high tea' route with finger sandwiches, scones and petits fours, or the 'comfort food' route with toad in the hole, sausage rolls and fish 'n' chips, one thing's for sure: you need some Union Jack decorations dotted around the room. Bunting, straws, napkins, plates, cushions, tablecloths… anything goes. You could even pin up some quintessentially English 'Keep Calm' posters related to food – like the one that says 'Keep Calm and Pub Lunch'. You could also buy some cardboard masks of the royal family, which you can give to guests as they arrive to wear throughout the night. They would never have guessed that when you suggested a movie night they'd be dining with the Queen!

IT'S MOVIE NIGHT!

Bridget Jones's Diary, This is England, Watership Down, Love Actually, Withnail and I, Notting Hill, The 39 Steps, Four Weddings and a Funeral, Trainspotting, Great Expectations, Lock, Stock and Two Smoking Barrels, A Fish Called Wanda, Monty Python and the Holy Grail, The Third Man, Snatch, Calendar Girls, The Full Monty, Mary Poppins, Oliver!, Carry On Doctor, Miss Potter, Billy Elliot, Mr. Toad's Wild Ride, Alice's Adventures in Wonderland, Wallace & Gromit in The Curse of the Were-Rabbit.

NUTTY POPCORN

Dig into this popcorn mingled with caramel-coated nuts as you watch Oompa-Loompas shake their thing, Augustus Gloop roll into a river of chocolate and Violet Beauregarde transform into a giant blueberry in *Charlie and the Chocolate Factory*. The only question is: were these nuts cracked by the trained squirrels coveted by Veruca Salt?

1–2 tablespoons sunflower or vegetable oil

90 g/⅓ cup popcorn kernels

225 g/1 cup plus 2 tablespoons (caster) sugar

2 teaspoons vanilla extract

250 g/8 oz. mixed unsalted roasted nuts (such as pecans, peanuts, almonds, macadamias)

Makes 1 large bowl

Heat the oil in a large lidded saucepan with a few popcorn kernels in the pan. When you hear the kernels pop, carefully tip in the rest of the kernels. Shake the pan over the heat until the popping stops. Take care when lifting the lid, as any unpopped kernels may still pop from the heat of the pan. Tip the popcorn into a bowl, removing any unpopped kernels as you go. To make the caramel nuts, put the sugar, vanilla extract and 125 ml/½ cup water in a small saucepan set over medium heat. Simmer until the sugar dissolves and you have a thin syrup. Add the mixed nuts to the pan and cook, without stirring, until the sugar caramelizes – this will take about 20 minutes and will happen suddenly. Remove the pan from the heat and stir the nuts well to make sure they are evenly coated in the caramel. Add the nuts and any loose sugar crystals to the popcorn and stir through. This popcorn can be served warm or cold.

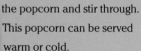

POSH PIMM'S

An English summer wedding wouldn't be the same without a glass of fruity Pimm's to sip. And a movie night screening the hilarious *Four Weddings and a Funeral* wouldn't be the same without four glasses of the same refreshment!

Allow 250 ml/1 cup per drink, and at least 2 drinks per person.

1 part Pimm's
3 parts ginger ale, lemonade or soda
borage flowers
curls of cucumber peel
sliced lemons
sprigs of fresh mint
Serves 1 or a party

Put all the ingredients into a jug/pitcher of ice, stir and serve.

HUGH GRANT

ANDIE MACDOWELL

A MIKE NEWELL FILM

four Weddings and a funeral

FIVE GOOD REASONS TO STAY SINGLE.

SAUSAGE ROLLS

375 g/13 oz. ready-rolled puff pastry
1 tablespoon Dijon mustard
24 cocktail sausages
1 egg, lightly beaten
baking sheet, lined with nonstick parchment paper
Makes 24

Sausage rolls are the perfect picnic food, so lay a rug on your lounge floor and host an indoor picnic party, complete with wicker hamper, plastic plates, cups, knives and forks, and whatever other finger foods you decide to serve.

Preheat the oven to 190°C (375°F) Gas 5. Sprinkle a little flour on a clean work surface. Unroll the pastry, and if it's thicker than 2 mm/⅛ inch, use a rolling pin to make it the right thickness. Spread the mustard over the pastry. With the long side of the pastry nearest to you, cut the pastry vertically into 6 equal strips. Cut each strip into 4. Place a sausage on each piece of pastry and roll the pastry around it. Arrange on the prepared baking sheet. Score 2 or 3 small cuts in the top of each sausage roll with a sharp knife and brush with the beaten egg. Put the baking sheet on the middle shelf of the preheated oven and bake for 30 minutes or until golden.

MR TOAD IN THE HOLE

Sausages surrounded by fluffy Yorkshire pudding is like a huge hug on a plate. Demolish this delight while watching *Mr. Toad's Wild Ride* and prepare to curse those Weasels with a full, satisfied belly.

115 g/1 cup plain/all-purpose flour
a pinch of salt
a pinch of ground black pepper
2 large eggs
250 ml/1 cup milk
a small bunch of fresh chives, snipped into
   2.5-cm/1-inch pieces with kitchen scissors
12 cocktail sausages

4 tablespoons
   vegetable oil
12-hole large muffin pan
Serves 4–6

Preheat the oven to 220°C (425°F) Gas 7. To make the batter, put the flour, salt and pepper in a large bowl. Make a hollow in the centre, then break the eggs into the hollow. Pour the milk into the hollow. Using a wire whisk, beat the eggs with the milk. Start to mix the flour into the hollow. When all the flour has been mixed in, whisk the batter well to get rid of any lumps. Add the snipped chives and whisk them into the batter. Using kitchen scissors, snip the links between the sausages. Put 1 teaspoon of oil into each hole of the muffin pan, then put it into the oven to heat. Remove the pan from the oven after 5 minutes – the oil will be very, very hot – and put it on a heatproof work surface. Carefully put 1 sausage in each hole, then put the pan back in the oven for 5 minutes. Pour or ladle the batter into a large jug/pitcher and stir it once or twice. Carefully remove the hot pan as before, then stand back (the oil can splutter) and carefully pour the batter into each hole so each one is half full. Gently replace the pan in the oven and bake for 20 minutes until golden brown and crispy. Remove from the oven and ease each toad out of its hole with a round-bladed knife. Serve immediately.

MINI FISH 'N' CHIPS

It doesn't get any more British than fish and chips… and it doesn't get any more entertaining than *A Fish Called Wanda*. This heist-comedy is the perfect film to tuck into while feasting on this GB dish. Poor Wanda!

6 large potatoes, thinly sliced
500 g/1 lb. 2 oz. salmon fillet,
cut into thin strips
vegetable oil, for frying
Batter
40 g/¼ cup cornflour/cornstarch
40 g/¼ cup plain/all purpose
flour

1 teaspoon baking powder
5 teaspoons vegetable oil
175 ml/¾ cup soda water or beer
newspaper and parchment paper
Serves 20

Assemble all the ingredients for the batter, but do not mix. Fill a wok one-third full of oil and heat to 190°C (375°F). Alternatively, fill a deep-fryer with oil and heat to the recommended temperature. Add the potato strips in batches and fry for about 2 minutes until creamy coloured. Remove with a slotted spoon and spread out to drain on crumpled paper towels. When all the chips are fried, reheat the oil and fry them again until crisp and golden. Drain on crumpled kitchen paper/paper towels and keep them warm in the oven. They should be so crisp that they rustle together. Skim the oil and reheat to 190°C (375°F). Put a large bowl to the left of the wok (if you're right-handed) and a serving platter lined with crumpled kitchen paper/paper towels to the right. Have the fish to the left of the

bowl. Put the batter ingredients into the bowl and mix quickly with chopsticks, leaving as lumpy as possible, and with a rim of flour left unmixed around the bowl. Using a pair of long chopsticks or tongs, dip each piece of fish quickly into the batter, then place gently in the hot oil. Fry until golden, then remove and drain on crumpled paper towels. To serve, make 20 paper cones by twisting a strip of parchment paper inside a strip of newspaper. Put a pinch of the chips into each cone and add a piece of fish. Make sure all the ingredients are lined up vertically, so people don't drop any on the floor. Serve immediately. You may need to reheat these a little – put them in the oven, in the paper cones, and heat with the oven door open for a few minutes. No longer or the paper will get too hot.

ROAST RABBIT WITH HERBS & CIDER

Various British films depict some nasty, vicious rabbits –
Watership Down, *Monty Python and the Holy Grail*, *Wallace & Gromit
In The Curse of the Were-Rabbit* – so as you and your guests are
enjoying this supper, imagine you're feasting on these beasts,
rather than cute Peter Rabbit or Benjamin Bunny in *Miss Potter*.

**4 wild rabbits, about
500 g/1 lb 2 oz. each or
2 farmed ones**
1 onion, chopped
1 carrot, sliced
1 bay leaf
12 streaky bacon slices
100 g/scant 1 stick butter
**3 tip sprigs of fresh
rosemary, or 1 long
one, broken into 3**
**6–8 tip sprigs of thyme,
2–3 whole sprigs**
**200 ml/¾ cup (hard)
cider**
**2 tablespoons double/
heavy cream (optional)**
**sea salt and freshly
ground black pepper**
instant-read thermometer
Serves 4

First cut the legs and saddle off
each rabbit and reserve with the
kidneys. To make a stock, put the bones in a saucepan, add the onion, carrot
and bay leaf, cover with water and simmer for about 1 hour. Strain off and
reserve the stock, discard the bones and reserve the onion and carrot. Preheat
the oven to 230°C (450°F) Gas 8. Loosen the tough membrane around the
saddles by sliding the point of a sharp knife along the backbone from under
the neck end to the tail, freeing the meat underneath. Do one side at a time,
then cut off and discard it. Cover the saddle with strips of bacon. Melt the
butter in a frying pan, add the legs and fry for about 5 minutes to give them a
bit of colour. Season with salt, pepper, and the rosemary and thyme. Put the
reserved onion and carrot in a roasting pan and set the legs and saddle on top.
Roast in the middle of a preheated oven for 15–20 minutes according to size.
Meanwhile, add the kidneys to the pan used to brown the legs, adding a little
extra butter if necessary. Fry gently until firm, then remove and set aside until
serving time. Deglaze the pan with the cider, add the stock and the cream (if
using) and reduce the gravy to increase the flavour and thicken it. Add salt and
pepper to taste. Arrange the meat and kidneys on a serving dish and pour the
sauce over the top.

ALICE'S SCRUMPTIOUS SCONES

Make like Alice and her kooky friends in the 1972 version of *Alice's Adventures in Wonderland* and host a 'mad' tea party, including these scrumptious scones. Make little 'Eat Me' and 'Drink Me' tags to attach to whatever you serve.

225 g/1¾ cups self-raising/
   self rising flour
1 teaspoon baking powder
2 tablespoons (caster) sugar
50 g/4 tablespoons butter, diced
75 ml/5 tablespoons milk

1 egg
thick cream and strawberry jam,
to serve
a 5-cm/2-inch round cookie cutter
baking sheet, lined with nonstick
parchment paper
Makes 10–12

Preheat the oven to 220°C (425°F) Gas 7. Put the flour, baking powder and sugar in a food processor and pulse to combine. Add the butter and process for about 20 seconds until the mixture resembles fine breadcrumbs. Tip the

mixture into a large bowl and make a hollow in the centre. Beat together the egg and milk and reserve 1 tablespoon of the mixture. Pour the remaining mixture into the flour and work in using a fork. Turn out on to a clean, floured work surface and knead briefly to make a soft, smooth dough. (Work in a little more flour if the mixture is sticky.) Pat out the dough to a thickness of about 2.5 cm/1 inch and stamp out rounds using the cookie cutter. Put the rounds on the prepared baking sheet, spacing them slightly apart. Brush with the reserved egg and milk mixture and bake in the oven for about 8 minutes until risen and golden. Transfer to a wire rack and let cool slightly. Serve split open and spread with cream and jam.

CLASSIC VICTORIA SPONGE

'I'm not a total dead loss as a woman. I can't knit or make plum jam but I can bake a bloody Victoria sponge. Course, I didn't actually bake this one – I got it at Marks & Spencer,' says Chris (Helen Mirren) from *Calendar Girls*. There'll be no need to cheat with this easy-peasy recipe – and yours will be even more delicious than a store-bought special.

180 g/1½ sticks butter, softened
180 g/¾ cup plus 2 tablespoons
  (caster) sugar
3 eggs
180 g/1⅓ cups plus 1 tablespoon
  self-raising/self-rising flour
3½ tablespoons raspberry jam

140 g/1¼ cups fresh raspberries
125 ml/½ cup whipping cream
icing/confectioners' sugar,
  for dusting

two 20-cm/8-inch sandwich pans,
greased and lined
Serves 8

Preheat the oven to 180°C (350°F) Gas 4. Put the butter and sugar in a bowl and beat together until pale and fluffy. Beat in the eggs one at a time. Sift in the flour and mix to combine. Spoon the cake batter into the prepared pans and level the surface using the back of the spoon. Bake in the preheated oven for 20–25 minutes until golden brown and the centre of the sponge springs back when lightly pressed. Turn the cakes out onto a wire rack, gently peel off the lining paper and let cool completely. To serve, spread the jam over one cake and top with the raspberries. Whip the cream until it stands in soft peaks, then spread it over the raspberries. Put the second cake on top and dust with icing/confectioners' sugar.

This
short cigar
belongs to
a man with
no name.

This
long gun
belongs to
a man with
no name.

This
poncho
belongs to
a man with
no name.

He's going to trigger a whole new style in adventure.

WESTERN

'In the cool of the evening, when the food and liquor and women are ready, that's when I appear' — *The Virginian*

Saddle up, people, it's time to round up your favourite cowboys and cowgirls for the culinary ride of your life, courtesy of your western-themed movie night – perhaps hosted at high noon. Encourage guests to don an Old Wild West get-up that includes a Stetson hat, cowboy boots, a checked shirt, a big belt buckle and anything else that screams 'yee-haw!' If you want to provide name badges, you could use sheriff-stars. In terms of decorations, some strategically placed cactus plants and cowboy-boot vases would be very effective. Grab your sewing machine by the horns and whip up a tablecloth made from bandanas. If you're in need of props, visit your local party store, which will most likely be packed with Western-themed paraphernalia. You could convert your living room into a gritty saloon with bullet-hole stickers, toy guns, playing cards, lassos, horseshoes, saddles, haystacks and 'Wanted' posters with photos of various 'outlaw' guests dotted around. You could even buy a western saloon curtain and hang it by the front door so people get a real sense of moseying into a new world when they arrive. A rootin', tootin' good time will be had by all.

IT'S MOVIE NIGHT!

True Grit, The Man Who Shot Liberty Valance, The Good, the Bad and the Ugly, The Virginian, Maverick, A Fistful of Dollars, The Magnificent Seven, City Slickers, Unforgiven, A Distant Trumpet, The Quick and the Dead, Tombstone, The Alamo, Once Upon a Time in the West, Back to the Future Part III, El Dorado, Wyatt Earp, Butch Cassidy and the Sundance Kid, The Searchers, Young Guns.

POPCORN NACHOS

1–2 tablespoons sunflower
  or vegetable oil
50 g/2 tablespoons
  popcorn kernels

Avocado salsa

2 beefsteak tomatoes
1 small shallot, finely
  chopped
2 ripe avocados, peeled,
  pitted and chopped
juice of 1 lime
1 tablespoon finely
  chopped fresh basil
2 tablespoons finely
  chopped fresh
  coriander/cilantro
1 teaspoon hot paprika
1 teaspoon (caster) sugar
sea salt and freshly
  ground black pepper

To serve

150 ml/⅔ cup sour cream
100 g/scant 1 cup grated
  Cheddar cheese

Serves 4–6

The Magnificent Seven is a great film to accompany this snack, which sees seven brave gunfighters protecting a Mexican village threatened by bandits. A snack with bang!

Heat the oil in a large lidded saucepan with a few popcorn kernels in the pan. When you hear the kernels pop, carefully tip in the rest of the kernels. Shake the pan over the heat until the popping stops. Take care when lifting the lid as any unpopped kernels may still pop from the heat of the pan. Tip the popcorn into a serving dish, removing any unpopped kernels as you go. To make the salsa, cut the tomatoes in half and discard the seeds and juice. Chop the tomato flesh into small pieces and put in a bowl with the chopped shallot, avocado and the lime juice. Stir so that the avocado is thoroughly coated in the lime juice (this will prevent discolouration). Add the chopped basil and coriander/cilantro, paprika and sugar, season well with salt and pepper and stir again. Drain the salsa in a sieve/strainer to remove any excess liquid. Make a hollow in the popcorn and pour the salsa into the centre of the dish. Top with the sour cream and sprinkle with the grated cheese. Place under a hot grill/broiler for about 5 minutes until the cheese melts and is bubbling, taking care that the popcorn does not burn. Remove from the grill/broiler and serve immediately.

LYNCHBURG LEMONADE

Made from good old southern bourbon whiskey, this is the ultimate cowboys' cocktail. Be careful not to drink too many or you could end up getting thrown through a window by the town's passing outlaw.

2 lemon wedges
2 barspoons (caster) sugar
50 ml/1¾ oz. Jack Daniel's
lemonade, to top up
Serves 1

Muddle the lemon and sugar together in a highball glass. Add ice and the remaining ingredients. Stir and serve.

BABY BACK RIBS

These sugar-rubbed baby back ribs with smoky barbecue sauce would have gone down a storm in the barbecue scene in *Giant*, starring Elizabeth Taylor, Rock Hudson and James Dean.

1½ teaspoons chilli/chili powder

1 teaspoon garlic salt

1 tablespoon sugar

1 teaspoon each salt and freshly ground black
  pepper

3 large racks of baby pork spareribs

Smoky barbecue sauce

1 tablespoon olive oil

1 small onion, diced

2 garlic cloves, chopped

2 dry-cured bacon slices, chopped

400-g/14-oz. can whole plum tomatoes, puréed

4 tablespoons tomato purée/paste

175 ml/¾ cup cider vinegar

125 g/heaped ½ cup brown sugar

2 tablespoons chilli/chili powder

2 teaspoons celery salt

3 tablespoons Worcestershire sauce

1 tablespoon yellow American mustard

2 teaspoons Spanish paprika

1 tablespoon chopped chipotle chillies/chiles in
  adobo, or Tabasco Sauce

Serves 4

Preheat the oven to 150°C (300°F) Gas 2. In a small bowl, mix together the chilli/chili powder, garlic salt, sugar, salt and pepper. Sprinkle the racks of pork on both sides with the mixture, put on a baking sheet and cook for 1½ hours. In the meantime, make the smoky barbecue sauce. Heat the olive oil in a medium saucepan. Sauté the onion, garlic and bacon for 5 minutes, or until soft. Add the remaining ingredients and cook for 10 minutes. If you are not using it straightaway, let cool and refrigerate in a sealed container. When you are ready to cook the ribs, light your barbecue or preheat a gas grill/broiler. Brush the ribs on both sides with the fresh barbecue sauce. Grill/broil or barbecue for 5 minutes on each side or until crispy around the edges.

BLAZING BAKED BEANS

If you're serving up maple baked beans, perhaps you should consider your guest list first. Does everyone know each other well? If the evening goes anything like the famous 'fart scene' in *Blazing Saddles*, you'll want everyone to feel comfortable enough in front of one another to parp away with gusto.

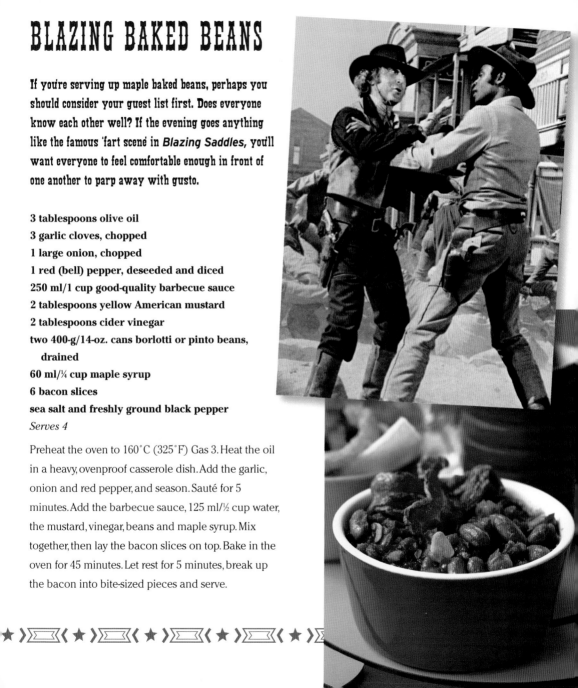

3 tablespoons olive oil
3 garlic cloves, chopped
1 large onion, chopped
1 red (bell) pepper, deseeded and diced
250 ml/1 cup good-quality barbecue sauce
2 tablespoons yellow American mustard
2 tablespoons cider vinegar
two 400-g/14-oz. cans borlotti or pinto beans,
    drained
60 ml/¼ cup maple syrup
6 bacon slices
sea salt and freshly ground black pepper
Serves 4

Preheat the oven to 160°C (325°F) Gas 3. Heat the oil in a heavy, ovenproof casserole dish. Add the garlic, onion and red pepper, and season. Sauté for 5 minutes. Add the barbecue sauce, 125 ml/½ cup water, the mustard, vinegar, beans and maple syrup. Mix together, then lay the bacon slices on top. Bake in the oven for 45 minutes. Let rest for 5 minutes, break up the bacon into bite-sized pieces and serve.

★)▷◁(★)▷◁(★)▷◁(★)▷◁(★)▷

COWBOY'S CORNED BEEF HASH

The perfect cowboy feast, you can just imagine the likes of Gary Cooper and Clint Eastwood shooting the shiz and chewing tobacco around a campfire as this one-skillet dinner sizzles and spits in front of them.

3 baking potatoes, diced
40 g/3 tablespoons butter
1 onion, diced
1 garlic clove, finely chopped
300 g/10½ oz. cooked corned
  beef brisket, diced

½ teaspoon Tabasco sauce
1 tablespoon vegetable oil
4 eggs
sea salt and freshly ground black
  pepper
Serves 4

Boil the potatoes in salted water for 6 minutes, drain and put them in a large bowl. Heat 15 g/1 tablespoon of the butter in a large, heavy-based frying pan. Add the onion, garlic and corned beef. Season and sauté for 5 minutes. Pour the mixture into the bowl with the potatoes. Add the Tabasco and mix well. Add the remaining butter to the pan. Pour the potato mixture into it and press everything down firmly. Cover with a heavy lid or plate that will fit just inside the pan to weight the mixture down. Cook over medium heat for 10 minutes. Turn the mixture over in batches and cook for 10 minutes on the other side. The meat should be brown and crisp. Keep cooking and turning if it isn't. Make 4 indentations in the potatoes and crack an egg into each. Put a fitted lid over the pan and cook until the eggs are done. Alternatively, in a separate nonstick frying pan, heat the vegetable oil and fry the eggs. Put one fried egg on top of each serving of corned beef hash. You can also poach the eggs instead of frying them, if you prefer.

This short cigar belongs to a man with no name.

This long gun belongs to a man with no name.

This poncho belongs to a man with no name.

He's going to trigger a whole new style in adventure.

PULLED PORK SANDWICH

Picture this: you've been in the saddle all day riding in the searing sun, you arrive into Dodge City and are ready to raise hell. Except, you're hungry. What would be the perfect grub to fill your belly and prepare you for some savage gunslinging? Why, a pulled pork sandwich, of course.

1 kg/2¼ lbs. boneless pork shoulder with fat

3 tablespoons olive oil

2 teaspoons smoked paprika

2 teaspoons dried oregano

1 teaspoon each salt and freshly ground black pepper

250 ml/1 cup good-quality barbecue sauce

To serve

4 crusty white rolls

ready-made coleslaw (optional)

Serves 4

Preheat the oven to 120°C (250°F) Gas ½. Rub the pork with 2 tablespoons of the olive oil and sprinkle with the paprika, oregano, salt and pepper. Heat a nonstick frying pan until very hot. Sear the pork on all sides and then put it in a roasting pan. Cook for 5 hours. Carefully remove the fat from the pork and shred the meat with 2 forks. Pour the barbecue sauce into a large frying pan. Add the shredded meat and warm through over medium heat. When ready to serve, scoop the meat into the rolls and serve with ready-made coleslaw, if liked.

TEXAS WHOOPIE PIE

125 g/1 stick butter,
softened
200 g/1 cup dark brown
sugar
1 large egg
1 tablespoon maple syrup
320 g/2½ cups self-
raising/self-rising flour
1 teaspoon baking
powder
½ teaspoon salt
250 ml/1 cup sour cream
100 ml/scant ½ cup hot
water

Maple glaze
60 g/⅓ cup dark brown
sugar
100 ml/scant ½ cup
maple syrup
2 tablespoons corn syrup
25 g/2 tablespoons
unsalted butter

Praline cream filling
75 g/½ cup pecans
100 g/½ cup (caster)
sugar
300 ml/1¼ cups double/
heavy cream, whipped
to stiff peaks

two 12-hole whoopie pie
pans, greased
piping bag fitted with a
large round nozzle/tip
Makes 12

The state tree of Texas is the pecan. Rejoice in this smooth brown nut with a whoopie pie and a couple of films set in Texas – like *The Alamo* and *Rio Bravo*.

Preheat the oven to 180°C (350°F) Gas 4. To make the pies, cream together the butter and brown sugar in a mixing bowl for 2–3 minutes using an electric hand-held mixer until light and creamy. Add the egg and maple syrup and mix again. Sift the flour and baking powder into the bowl and add the salt and sour cream. Whisk again until everything is incorporated. Add the hot water and whisk into the mixture. Put a large spoonful of mixture into each hole of the prepared pans. Let stand for 10 minutes, then bake each pan in the preheated oven for 10–12 minutes. Remove the pies from the oven, let cool slightly, then turn out onto a wire rack. To make the maple glaze, put the sugar, maple syrup, corn syrup and butter in a saucepan set over gentle heat and warm until the sugar has melted. Drizzle over 12 of the pie halves. This is best done while the pies are still warm and on the wire rack, with parchment paper underneath to catch any drips. Let cool completely. To make the praline cream filling, sprinkle the pecans over a sheet of parchment paper, selecting 12 halves to use for decoration. Warm the sugar in a saucepan set over gentle heat until melted and golden. Do not stir but watch very closely, as it will burn easily. As the sugar starts to melt, swirl the pan. When melted, use a spoon to drizzle the caramel over all of the pecans, swirling lacy patterns over the pecans selected for decoration. Once cooled, set the decoration pecans to one side and blitz the remaining ones to a fine dust in a food processor. Fold this praline powder into the whipped cream. Spoon the cream into the prepared piping bag and pipe circles of it onto the unglazed pie halves. Top with the glazed pie halves and finish each one with a caramel pecan.

ALL-AMERICAN APPLE PIE

As American as John Wayne, apple pie was the inspiration behind the name of a small town in New Mexico - Pie Town. With its striking red rocks and vast, dramatic scenery, New Mexico has been the backdrop to countless western movies, including *A Distant Trumpet*, *City Slickers* and *The Outlaw*.

500 g/1 lb. 2 oz. ready-made
  shortcrust pastry
6 Granny Smith apples, peeled,
  cored and thinly sliced
6 Golden Delicious apples, peeled,
  cored and sliced ½ cm thick
165 g/¾ cup plus 1 tablespoon
  (caster) sugar
2½ tablespoons cornflour/
  cornstarch
1 teaspoon grated lemon zest

1 tablespoon lemon juice
1 teaspoon ground
  cinnamon
¼ teaspoon ground cloves
½ teaspoon grated nutmeg
½ teaspoon salt
1 egg white
23-cm/9-inch round
pie dish
Serves 8

Roll out half the pastry on a clean, floured work surface and arrange in the pie dish. Set aside. Roll out the other half to a 30-cm/12-inch disc. Transfer to a piece of parchment paper. Chill in the fridge for at least 1 hour before filling. Preheat the oven to 190°C (375°F) Gas 5. Put a baking sheet inside to heat. To make the filling, toss the apples in a mixing bowl with 150 g/¾ cup of the sugar, the cornflour/cornstarch, lemon zest and juice, cinnamon, cloves, nutmeg and salt. Pour into the uncooked pie shell and cover with the rolled pastry. Press the edges together to seal. Crimp the edges of the pastry in a zigzag pattern. Cut 4 small slits in the top of the pie with a knife to let the steam out. Brush the top with the egg white and sprinkle over the remaining tablespoon of sugar. Bake the pie on the hot baking sheet for 60 minutes or until golden brown.

A WARNER
BROS.
PICTURE

CASABLANCA

The Golden Age

'Fiddle-dee-dee! Ashley Wilkes told me he likes to see a girl with a healthy appetite!' – *Gone With The Wind*

The elegance, the chivalry, the love, the laughs… Relive the golden age of Hollywood by screening timeless tales while serving classic cocktails, canapés and cupcakes. Yes, it's time to get your vintage on with the likes of Ingrid Bergman, Humphrey Bogart and Marilyn Monroe. Urge guests to dress appropriately to pay homage to the period – the iconic grace of the era really won't be set off with jeans and a t-shirt. For guys, think lounge suits, bowties and spiffy hats; for women, glamorous dresses, elaborate hairdos and sparkling jewellery. A fun game that you could play before you start the movie is 'What Film?' Read out memorable quotes from various films and ask people to identify the flick from which it originates. Extra points given if they can name the actor/actress or character who said it. Even more points given if they decide to then act out the scene.

IT'S SHOWTIME!

Casablanca, It's a Wonderful Life, Gone with the Wind, Some Like It Hot, Wuthering Heights, To Have and Have Not, Jezebel, All About Eve, From Here to Eternity, Singin' in the Rain, War and Peace, Seven Brides for Seven Brothers, Gigi, The Best Years of Our Lives, Gentlemen Prefer Blondes, National Velvet, Holiday Inn, Now, Voyager, A Streetcar Named Desire, Funny Face.

Lovers' Popcorn

1–2 tablespoons sunflower
or vegetable oil
90 g/⅓ cup popcorn
kernels
1 vanilla pod/bean
80 g/5½ tablespoons
butter
70 g/⅓ cup (caster) sugar
Makes 1 large bowl

Liven up regular popcorn with vanilla and you've got a seriously sweet treat on your hands. Mix in a classic tale of love — perhaps the madcap romance of Doris Day and Rock Hudson — and you're in for one heck of a night.

Heat the oil in a large lidded saucepan with a few popcorn kernels in the pan. When you hear the kernels pop, carefully tip in the rest of the kernels. Shake the pan over the heat until the popping stops. Take care when lifting the lid, as any unpopped kernels may still pop from the heat of the pan. Tip the popcorn into a bowl, removing any unpopped kernels as you go. Split the vanilla pod/bean lengthways and remove the seeds by running a round-bladed knife along both halves of the pod. Add the pod halves and seeds to a small saucepan with the butter and heat gently, stirring, until the butter has melted. Remove the vanilla pod/bean from the pan and pour the vanilla butter over the popcorn. Sprinkle over the sugar and stir well so that everything is evenly coated. This popcorn is delicious warm or cold.

Casablanca Cocktail

Who could forget the classic line uttered by Humphrey Bogart to Ingrid Bergman in *Casablanca* as they clink glasses: 'Here's looking at you, kid'? Enjoy your own goosebump-inducing moment with this royal gin fizz cocktail.

1 egg white
50 ml/1¾ oz. gin
25 ml/1 oz. lemon juice
1 barspoon sugar (or 15 ml/½ oz.
**   sugar syrup)**
champagne to top up
Serves 1

Put the egg white, gin, lemon juice and sugar into a shaker filled with ice and shake vigorously. Strain into a collins glass filled with ice. Top up with champagne.

A WARNER BROS. PICTURE

CASABLANCA

Davis Daiquiri

Bette Davis can be seen in many films with a drink in her hand (good lass), so raise a glass to this cocktail lover as you settle in to view *Now, Voyager*, *Jezebel*, or *All About Eve*, where she downs her drink and says, 'Fasten your seatbelts, it's going to be a bumpy night.'

50 ml/1¾ oz. golden rum
20 ml/¾ oz. lime juice
10 ml/2 barspoons sugar syrup
Serves 1

Pour all the ingredients into an ice-filled shaker. Shake and strain into a martini glass.

Cary Grant Canapés

Relish
**200 g/7 oz. cooked
beetroot/beet, finely
diced**
**1 large shallot, finely
chopped**
**1 tablespoon snipped
fresh chives**
**2 tablespoons tomato
purée/paste**
*Smoked haddock and
celeriac/celery root
topping*
**300 g/10 oz. smoked
haddock fillet**
**200 g/7 oz. celeriac/
celery root, peeled**
**3 tablespoons
mayonnaise**
**1 tablespoon horseradish
sauce**
**500 g/1 lb. 2 oz.
pumpernickel**
**fresh coriander/cilantro
leaves, to garnish
(optional)**
5-cm/2-inch round cookie
cutter
Makes 30–40

When hosting a Golden Era movie night, the name of the game is sophistication and class. Can you imagine the debonair Cary Grant sitting down to a burger and fries? Exactly. These smoked haddock and celeriac/celery root bites on pumpernickel bread will set the tone.

To make the relish, put all the ingredients in a bowl and mix to combine. Cover and refrigerate until needed. For the smoked haddock and celeriac/celery root topping, put the smoked haddock in a saucepan with just enough cold water to cover. Bring to the boil, reduce the heat and let simmer for about 2 minutes until cooked, then drain and flake (removing any skin and little bones). Let cool. Coarsely grate the celeriac/celery root or shred it in a food processor. Transfer to a bowl and stir in the mayonnaise, horseradish and flaked haddock. Cut the pumpernickel into 30–40 rounds using the cookie cutter or squares. Spoon a little haddock and celeriac mixture onto each one. Using a clean spoon, pile a little beetroot/beet relish on top and garnish with a coriander/cilantro leaf, if using. Serve immediately.

Guys and Dolls Pots

300 ml/1¼ cups single/
   light cream
300 ml/1¼ cups milk
100 g/1 cup finely grated
   Parmesan
4 egg yolks
cayenne pepper
12 anchovy fillets
50 g/4 tablespoons
   unsalted butter
8 very thin slices of
   rustic bread
sea salt and finely
   ground white pepper
8 ramekins, buttered
large ovenproof dish
Serves 8

Encourage your guests to sing along with Italian crooner Frank Sinatra in Guys and Dolls while you serve up this swish appetizer using delicious Italian ingredients.

Mix the cream, milk and all but 1 tablespoon of the Parmesan in a heatproof bowl, place it over a saucepan of boiling water and warm it gently until the Parmesan has melted. Remove the bowl from on top of the pan and let cool completely. Preheat the oven to 150°C (300°F) Gas 2. Whisk the egg yolks, a pinch of salt, a pinch of white pepper and a little cayenne pepper into the cool cream mixture, then pour into the prepared ramekins. Place the ramekins in an ovenproof dish in the oven, then pour boiling water into the dish to reach halfway up the ramekins. Cover the whole dish with a sheet of buttered parchment paper and bake in the preheated oven for 15 minutes or until the custards have just set. Remove from the oven and turn on the grill/broiler. Mash the anchovies and butter to make a smooth paste and spread over 4 of the slices of bread. Cover with the remaining bread and toast in a sandwich toaster or panini machine. Sprinkle the remaining Parmesan over the warm custards and brown gently under the hot grill/broiler. Cut the toasted anchovy sandwiches into fingers and serve with the pots.

Golden Age Meringues

These mini meringues brushed with chocolate are easy, elegant and effortlessly chic – perfect to complement a classic cocktail and canapés.

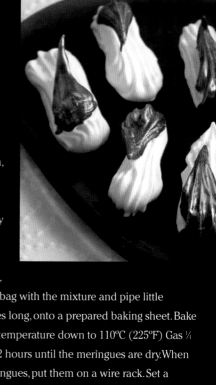

3 egg whites
¼ teaspoon cream of
tartar
170 g/¾ cup plus 1
tablespoons (caster)
sugar
200 g/7 oz. dark/
semisweet chocolate,
broken into small
pieces
gold edible paint or
edible glitter (optional)
piping bag with a fluted
nozzle/tip
2 baking sheets lined with
nonstick parchment paper
Makes 40–50

Preheat the oven to 130°C (250°F) Gas ½. Put the egg whites in a clean, grease-free bowl and beat with an electric whisk until stiff. Add the cream of tartar and beat again. Very slowly add the sugar, beating constantly, until all the sugar is incorporated and you have a thick, glossy, silky mixture. Fill the piping bag with the mixture and pipe little 'tongues', each about 7 cm/3 inches long, onto a prepared baking sheet. Bake for 30 minutes, then turn the oven temperature down to 110°C (225°F) Gas ¼ and continue baking for a further 2 hours until the meringues are dry. When you are ready to decorate the meringues, put them on a wire rack. Set a heatproof bowl over a pan of barely simmering water, making sure the bowl does not touch the water. Put the chocolate in the base of the bowl and let melt slowly. When it has melted, gently brush a lick of dark chocolate down the length of each meringue using a soft pastry brush. Leave to cool and set, then smudge on a little gold edible paint, if liked, and serve.

Walk of Fame Cookies

Pay tribute to the classic Hollywood stars by nibbling on these cookies. Why not pipe the name of a star onto each one and watch guests scramble for their best-loved idol, be it Ginger Rogers, Judy Garland or James Dean?

140 g/1¼ sticks butter,
    softened
100 g/¾ cup icing/
    confectioners' sugar
1 drop vanilla extract
1 egg yolk
200 g/1½ cups plain/
    all-purpose flour
30 g/⅓ cup ground
    almonds
silver leaf, to decorate
2 baking sheets, greased
star shaped cookie cutters
Makes 20 cookies

Using a hand-held electric whisk, beat together the butter, icing/confectioners' sugar and vanilla until creamy. Add the egg yolk and beat well. Stir in the flour and ground almonds (if using) and quickly mix to a firm dough using your hands. Knead into a ball, then lightly flatten. Wrap the dough in clingfilm/plastic wrap and chill in the fridge for 2–3 hours. Preheat the oven to 180°C (350°F) Gas 4. Turn the dough onto a clean, lightly floured work surface and roll out using a rolling pin. Using star-shaped cookie cutters, stamp out as many cookies as you can from the dough. Arrange the cookies on the prepared baking sheets. Bake for about 8 minutes, or until firm and light golden brown. Remove from the oven and let the cookies settle for 1 minute before removing with a palette knife onto a wire rack. To decorate with silver leaf, brush the surface of the cookies with a pastry brush lightly dampened with water. Let the area become tacky. Using tweezers, transfer pieces of silver leaf onto the star cookies to create a mottled silver effect.

Sparkling Diamond Cupcakes

Cupcakes are a girl's best friend! These dazzling desserts are ideal to indulge in while soaking up the performances of shimmering starlets like Marilyn Monroe and Mae West.

Preheat the oven to 180°C (350°F) Gas 4. Beat the butter and sugar together in a bowl until pale and fluffy, then beat in the eggs, one at a time. Sift the flour into the mixture and fold in, then stir in the ginger and lime zest. Spoon the mixture into the paper cases, then bake in the preheated oven for about 17 minutes until risen and golden and a skewer inserted in the centre comes out clean. Transfer to a wire rack and let cool completely. To decorate, leave the mints in their wrappers and tap with a rolling pin to break into pieces. Set aside. Put the lime juice in a bowl, then sift the icing/confectioners' sugar into the bowl and stir until smooth.

125 g/1 stick butter,
   softened
115 g/½ cup plus 1
   tablespoon sugar
2 eggs
115 g/1 cup self-raising/
   self-rising flour
3 pieces of stem ginger in
   syrup, drained and
   chopped
grated zest of 1 lime
To decorate
about 6 clear mints
2½ tablespoons lime juice
200 g/1½ cups icing/
   confectioners' sugar
pale blue food colouring
edible clear sparkles
a 12-hole cupcake pan,
lined with silver cupcake
cases

Makes 12

Add a little more lime juice as required to make a smooth, spoonable icing. Add a couple of drops of food colouring and stir in to achieve a pale blue colour. Spoon the icing on top of the cakes. Pile a little heap of mint 'diamonds' on each cake and sprinkle with edible sparkles.

RAY LIOTTA   ROBERT DE NIRO   JOE PESCI

As far back as I can remember I've always wanted
to be a gangster.

GoodFellas
A MARTIN SCORSESE PICTURE

Three Decades of Life in the Mafia

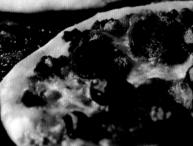

Mob Squad

'Leave the gun, take the cannoli' — *The Godfather*

Here's an offer your guests can't refuse: a gangster movie night with lip-smackingly delicious Italian fare. If there's one thing gangsters love, it's food – 'just like Mama used to make'. Remember in *Goodfellas* when Jimmy, Henry and Tommy stop by Tommy's house in the middle of a 'job' (leaving some guy bleeding in the car) and his Ma insists on fixing them all a full Italian dinner? Make like Ma and do the same for your guests, who hopefully won't be leaving afterwards to 'take care' of someone. Encourage guests to invent a gangster name for themselves – they could be Charlie 'Green Eyes' or Ben 'The Butcher', and invite them over for a 'sit-down', stressing the importance of keeping their arrival at your house on the down-low because you think the Feds are watching. If you really want to get into the spirit, before you start the film, you could play a murder mystery-esque game, but instead of people having to guess the murderer, they have to figure out who the 'rat' is. If *Casino* is on the agenda, perhaps you could set up a roulette, blackjack or poker table. Decorate the room with pictures of real-life gangsters like Al Capone, Mickey Cohen and the Kray brothers

IT'S SHOWTIME!

The Godfather Trilogy, Goodfellas, Scarface, King of New York, Donnie Brasco, Casino, Mean Streets, Once Upon a Time in America, Pulp Fiction, Reservoir Dogs, Heat, Bugsy Malone, L.A. Confidential, Gangster Squad, The Public Enemy, Road To Perdition, The Untouchables, Blow, The Departed, A Bronx Tale, Married to the Mob, The Usual Suspects, Layer Cake, Mickey Blue Eyes, American Gangster.

Public Enemy Popcorn

20 g/¾ oz. dried porcini
   mushrooms
90 g/⅓ cup popcorn
   kernels
1–2 tablespoons sunflower
   or vegetable oil
70 g/5 tablespoons butter
1 teaspoon black truffle
   salt or a drizzle of
   truffle oil and 1
   teaspoon sea salt

Makes 1 large bowl

The *Public Enemy* starring the
legendary James Cagney is based on
the real life story of street thugs in
Al Capone's prohibition-era Chicago,
based on a memoir called blood and
beer – so get some beer on ice and a
bowl of this delicious popcorn on your
lap and enjoy a forgotten classic!

In a food processor, blitz the mushrooms to a fine powder
and set aside. Heat the oil in a large lidded saucepan with
a few popcorn kernels in the pan. When you hear the
kernels pop, carefully tip in the rest of the kernels. Shake
the pan over the heat until the popping stops. Take care
when lifting the lid, as any unpopped kernels may still
pop from the heat of the pan. Tip the popcorn into a
bowl, removing any unpopped kernels as you go. Melt
the butter in a small saucepan set over medium heat
and pour over the warm popcorn. Sprinkle over the
mushroom powder and truffle salt and stir well so that
the popcorn is evenly coated. This popcorn is best
served warm.

Espresso Martini

It seems that espresso coffee is as synonymous with Italy as high fashion and the Pope. Put this classy cocktail in the hand of any woman and she'll instantly inspire the words, 'Ciao, bella.'

50 ml/1¾ oz. fresh espresso coffee
50 ml/1¾ oz. vodka
a dash of sugar syrup
3 coffee beans, to garnish
Serves 1

Pour the espresso coffee into a shaker, add the vodka and sugar syrup, shake the mixture sharply and strain into an old-fashioned glass filled with ice. Garnish with coffee beans.

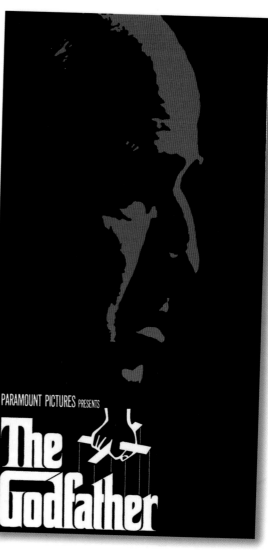

PARAMOUNT PICTURES PRESENTS

The Godfather

Scarface Crostini

'Say hello to my little toasts!' Tony 'Scarface' Montana supposedly lived the American Dream – coming from nothing and making something of himself, albeit transforming into a cocaine-addled nut job in the process. The final scene of this movie proves that if you crossed him, like this snack, you'd be toast.

1 focaccia

olive oil, for drizzling

sea salt and freshly ground
   black pepper

Garlic mushroom topping

1 tablespoon olive oil

15 g/1 tablespoon unsalted
   butter

1 shallot, finely chopped

250 g/8 oz. mixed wild
   mushrooms

1 tablespoon freshly chopped
   flat-leaf parsley

1 garlic clove, peeled

Mediterranean tomato topping

4 ripe tomatoes

1 roasted red pepper, from a jar

1 tablespoon fresh basil leaves,
   torn

1 tablespoon chopped mixed
   pitted olives

100 g/3½ oz. buffalo mozzarella,
   torn

1 garlic clove, peeled

Bean and mint topping

175 g/1⅓ cups cooked
   broad/fava beans and/or peas,
   crushed

1 tablespoon freshly chopped
   mint

grated zest of ½ lemon

100 g/3½ oz. feta, crumbled

1 garlic clove, peeled

20 x 30-cm/8 x 12-inch baking pan

Serves 4–6

Cut the focaccia into finger-width slices, toast both sides on a ridged stove-top griddle/grill pan and top with one of the following toppings. For the garlic mushroom topping, heat the oil and butter in a frying pan, add the shallot and cook over medium heat until translucent. Add the mushrooms, season, cook until tender and stir in the parsley. For the Mediterranean tomato topping, chop the tomatoes and red pepper. Add the basil and olives and gently stir in the mozzarella. For the bean and mint topping, cook the beans in lightly salted boiling water until tender. Drain and refresh under cold water. Drain well, then whizz in a food processor to a coarse purée. Stir in the mint, lemon zest and feta and season. To serve any of the toppings, rub the garlic clove over the toasted bread and pile the mixture on top. Drizzle with olive oil. Serve hot.

Kick-ass Arancini

These fried risotto balls coated in breadcrumbs are said to have originated in Sicily in the 10th century. When served at your movie night, you can explain to guests that they represent the gangsters' big 'cojones'! Without said 'cojones', would they really have had the guts to put someone's head in a vice or stab someone repeatedly in the neck with a pen?

15 g/½ oz. dried porcini
    mushrooms
1 tablespoon olive oil
25 g/2 tablespoons unsalted
    butter
2 shallots, finely chopped
1 fat garlic clove, crushed
250 g/1¼ cups risotto rice
750–850 ml/3–3½ cups hot
    vegetable stock

40 g/⅓ cup grated Pecorino
1 tablespoon freshly chopped
    flat-leaf parsley
125 g/4½ oz. mozzarella, diced
100 g/¾ cup plain/all-purpose
    flour
2 eggs, lightly beaten
200 g/4½ cups fresh, fine
    breadcrumbs
about 1 litre/4 cups sunflower

oil, for frying
sea salt and freshly ground
    black pepper
Makes 15–18

Soak the porcini in a small bowl of boiling water for about 15 minutes or until soft. Drain well on kitchen paper/paper towels and finely chop. Heat the olive oil and butter in a saucepan and add the shallots, garlic and chopped porcini. Cook over low–medium heat until soft but not coloured. Add the rice and stir to coat well. Gradually add the vegetable stock – add it one ladleful at a time, and as the stock is absorbed by the rice, add another ladleful, stirring as you do so. Continue cooking in this way until the rice is al dente. Remove from the heat, add the Pecorino and herbs and season well. Tip the risotto into a bowl and let cool completely. Once the rice is cold, divide it

into walnut-sized pieces and roll into balls. Taking one ball at a time, flatten it into a disc in the palm of your hand, press some diced mozzarella in the middle and wrap the rice around it to completely encase the cheese. Shape into a neat ball. Repeat with the remaining risotto. Tip the flour, beaten eggs and breadcrumbs into separate shallow bowls. Roll the rice balls first in the flour, then coat well in the eggs and finally, roll them in the breadcrumbs to completely coat. Pour oil to a depth of about 5 cm/2 inches into a deep saucepan. Heat until hot. Cook the arancini, in batches, in the hot oil for 3–4 minutes or until crisp, hot and golden brown.

Pizzette

4 ready-made mini
   pizza bases
Toppings
5 tablespoons olive oil
1 small aubergine/
   eggplant, thinly sliced
1 onion, thinly sliced
a pinch of fresh thyme
   leaves
4 generous teaspoons
   sun-dried tomato paste
75 g/½ cup cherry
   tomatoes, quartered
125 g/4½ oz. dolcelatte or
   gorgonzola, crumbled
8 slices of pepperoni
a handful of black olives
100 g/3½ oz. mozzarella,
   diced
2 teaspoons basil pesto
2 canned artichoke
   hearts, sliced
2 tablespoons semi-dried
   tomatoes
handful of wild
   rocket/arugula
sea salt and freshly
   ground black pepper
fresh basil leaves,
   to garnish
solid baking sheet
Makes 4 mini pizzas

Speciality pizzas fit for the *Goodfellas*, the assorted meat and vegetable toppings will satisfy your guests' appetites for sure. You could even assign each pizza the name of the tough-guy actors who starred in the movie – the Robert De Niro, the Joe Pesci, the Ray Liotta and the Paul Sorvino. The Joe Pesci would, of course, be the spiciest.

Heat 2 tablespoons of the oil in a frying pan and fry the aubergine/eggplant on both sides until golden, then remove from the heat. In another pan, heat the remaining olive oil and gently fry the onion until very tender and just starting to turn golden. Add the thyme and remove from the heat. Preheat the oven to 230°C (450°F) Gas 8. Put the pizza bases on the baking sheet, then spread sun-dried tomato paste over 2 of the pizzas. Top one pizza with the aubergine/eggplant slices, cherry tomatoes and half the crumbled dolcelatte. Top the other pizza with pepperoni, olives and half the diced mozzarella. For the third pizza, spread the basil pesto over the base and arrange the artichoke hearts and semi-dried tomatoes on top. Scatter the remaining mozzarella over it. Garnish with basil leaves. Top the last pizza with the sautéed onions and remaining dolcelatte. Season all the pizzas well and cook on the top shelf of the oven for about 5 minutes or until golden. Top the onion pizza with the rocket/arugula and serve immediately.

Mobster's Perfect Pizza

Chicago is well-known for pizza. A fair few mobster movies were set in Chicago, such as *The Untouchables* and *Road to Perdition*. Ergo, if you're screening these movies, your menu selection is a no-brainer.

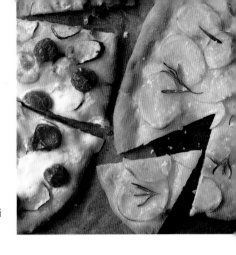

2 large ready-made pizza bases
Cherry tomato topping
2 courgettes/zucchini, thinly sliced
3 tablespoons olive oil
2 garlic cloves, crushed
200 g/1⅓ cups cherry tomatoes
1 large ball of fresh buffalo mozzarella, roughly torn
sea salt and freshly ground black pepper
Potato and rosemary topping
3 small, waxy new potatoes, very thinly sliced, ideally using a mandoline
2 tablespoons olive oil
2 garlic cloves, chopped
2 tablespoons fresh rosemary needles
sea salt
2 solid baking sheets
Each pizza serves 4

Preheat the oven to 230°C (450°F) Gas 8. To make the cherry tomato topping, put the courgettes/zucchini in a bowl with 2 tablespoons of the oil and the garlic. Season well with salt and pepper. Toss the courgettes/zucchini around until evenly coated in the garlicky oil. Arrange the courgettes/zucchini on one pizza base, along with the cherry tomatoes. Sprinkle the mozzarella pieces over the top and drizzle with the remaining oil. To make the potato and rosemary topping, put the potato slices in a bowl with the oil and garlic and season well with salt. Arrange them on the other pizza base, scatter with the rosemary needles and drizzle the garlicky oil from the bowl over the top. Put the baking sheets in the oven for 10–15 minutes until they are very hot. Carefully transfer the pizzas to the baking sheets and cook them in the preheated oven for about 20 minutes until the dough around the edges turns golden. (If your oven is not big enough to take both pizzas side by side, you can cook them on 2 shelves, but do swap them over after 10 minutes of cooking.) Use a spatula to lift them up to check that the bases are cooked golden. Serve immediately.

'Got A Beef' Lasagne

about 12 sheets dried
   lasagne
50 g/½ cup grated
   Parmesan cheese
Ragù
50 g/4 tablespoons butter
75 g/3 oz. pancetta or
   dry-cure smoked
   bacon, cubed
1 onion, finely chopped
1 carrot, chopped
1 celery stalk, chopped
250 g/9 oz. lean minced/
   ground beef
2 tablespoons tomato
   purée/paste
100 ml/scant ½ cup dry
   white wine
200 ml/¾ cup beef stock
freshly grated nutmeg
sea salt and freshly
   ground black pepper
Béchamel sauce
150 g/1⅓ sticks butter
110 g/¾ cup plus 2
   tablespoons
   plain/all-purpose flour
about 1 litre/4 cups milk
sea salt
20 x 25-cm/8 x 10-inch
baking dish, buttered
Serves 4–6

Just like the plotlines to mafia movies, this dish has many layers! The first layer is the meat (the gruesome 'whacking' of numerous people), the second layer is the pasta (the relationships between the wise guys) and the third layer is the cheese (the quotable phrases like 'sleeping with the fishes').

To make the ragù, melt the butter in a saucepan, add the cubed pancetta and cook for 2–3 minutes until browning. Add the onion, carrot and celery and cook for 5 minutes. Stir in the beef and brown until just changing colour, breaking it up with a wooden spoon. Add the tomato purée/paste, mix well and pour in the wine and stock. Season well with grated nutmeg, salt and pepper. Bring to the boil, cover and simmer very gently for as long as you can – 2 hours if possible. To make the béchamel sauce, melt the butter in a medium saucepan. When foaming, add the flour and cook over gentle heat for about 5 minutes without letting it brown. Turn off the heat and add all the milk at once, whisking very well. When all the flour and butter have been amalgamated and there are no lumps, return to the heat and slowly bring to the boil, whisking all the time. When it comes to the boil, add salt and simmer gently for 2–3 minutes. Cover the surface with clingfilm/plastic wrap to prevent a skin forming. Cook the sheets of dried lasagne in a large saucepan of boiling water in batches according to the package instructions. Lift out with a slotted spoon and drain on a clean dish towel. Preheat the oven to 180°C (350°F) Gas 4. Spoon one-third of the ragù into the buttered baking dish. Cover with 4 sheets of lasagne and spread with one-third of the béchamel sauce. Repeat twice more, finishing with a layer of béchamel sauce covering the whole top. Sprinkle with Parmesan. Bake in the preheated oven for about 45 minutes until brown and bubbling. Let stand for 10 minutes to settle and firm up before serving.

Tiramisu

300 g/1¼ cups
   mascarpone
3 tablespoons (caster)
   sugar
2 eggs, separated
300–350 g/10½–12 oz.
   soft amaretti
125 ml/½ cup cold
   espresso
1½ tablespoons Kahlúa
cocoa powder and
   finely grated chocolate,
   to sprinkle
4 serving dishes,
preferably glass
Serves 4

A typical Italian dessert, and a *Layer Cake* of sorts, tiramisu is a delectable treat to serve during your gangster film night. The mascarpone cheese is as cool and smooth as Daniel Craig and the rich, almond flavour is just as tasty too.

Put the mascarpone, sugar and egg yolks in a bowl and beat together until creamy. In a clean, grease-free bowl, whisk the egg whites until they form stiff peaks. Fold a couple of spoonfuls of the egg whites into the mascarpone mixture, then fold in the remaining egg whites, one-third at a time. Put a couple of spoonfuls of the mascarpone mixture into the base of 4 serving dishes and smooth the surface. Working carefully, soak about half the amaretti in the coffee for a minute or 2 until saturated (but not collapsing). Put a couple on top of the mascarpone, then sprinkle ¼–½ teaspoon Kahlúa over each serving. Continue layering with more mascarpone, coffee-soaked amaretti and Kahlúa, finishing with a layer of mascarpone. Dust with cocoa powder, then cover and chill in the fridge overnight. Sprinkle with cocoa powder and grated chocolate and serve.

SCHWARZENEGGE

Get ready for the ride
of your life.

TOTAL RECALL

May the force be with you

Sound Recorded with the DOLBY SYSTEM

Read the sensational novel in Sphere paperback

Sci-Fi

'Eat this' — *Total Recall*

I f you want your sci-fi movie night to be out of this world, it's time to get creative. Decorate the walls and ceiling with glow-in-the-dark stars, draw alien eyes on green balloons, lay out a silver tablecloth and serve food on 'spacy' plates and napkins, and wrap silver Christmas tinsel around anything and everything you can. You could even 'invite' an inflatable alien and have him sit between your guests during the film. If you want to play a few sci-fi-inspired games before the movie, how about 'pin the antenna on the alien' or 'bite the planet', which involves blindfolded guests trying to take a chomp out of doughnuts suspended from the ceiling by a piece of string. Play songs such as *Planet Claire* by The B-52s, *Aliens Exist* by Blink-182 and *Space Oddity* by David Bowie.

The recipes in this section encourage you to boldly go into the kitchen to produce some of the most galactic, creative culinary delights this universe has ever seen. May the fork be with you.

IT'S SHOWTIME!

Avatar, WALL-E, Independence Day, Gremlins, Star Wars, E.T. the Extra-Terrestrial, Starship Troopers, The Hitchhiker's Guide to the Galaxy, 2001: A Space Odyssey, Alien, Blade Runner, Metropolis, The Terminator, Planet of the Apes, Solaris, Forbidden Planet, Total Recall, The Matrix, TRON, The Thing, The Fifth Element, Back to the Future, Gattaca, Minority Report, Spaceballs.

Gremlin Popcorn

1–2 tablespoons sunflower
   or vegetable oil
90 g/⅓ cup popcorn
   kernels
70 g/5 tablespoons butter
zest and juice of 3 limes
80 g/scant ½ cup sugar
a few drops of green food
   colouring gel
1–2 tablespoons tequila
1 teaspoon flaked sea salt
Makes 1 large bowl

Surely a staple for the evil green monsters who loved to party, laugh manically, terrorize an entire town and, er, wear popcorn bags on their pointy ears.

Heat the oil in a large lidded saucepan with a few popcorn kernels in the pan. When you hear the kernels pop, carefully tip in the rest of the kernels. Shake the pan over the heat until the popping stops. Take care when lifting the lid, as any unpopped kernels may still pop from the heat of the pan. Tip the popcorn into a bowl, removing any unpopped kernels as you go. Melt the butter in a small saucepan set over gentle heat. Add the lime zest and juice and the sugar and simmer, stirring all the time, until the sugar has dissolved and you have a sticky syrup. Add a few drops of food colouring and stir to mix. Pour the lime syrup over the popcorn and stir so that all the kernels are evenly coated. Drizzle the tequila over, then crush the sea salt between your fingers, sprinkle over the popcorn and stir again. Serve warm or cold.

Blue Moon

Feel one step closer to the blue-skinned Na'vi tribe in Avatar as you sip this cocktail while watching them fight for their existence on Pandora, the moon that they call home.

50 ml/1¾ oz. Sauza Hornitos tequila
25 ml/1 oz. blue Curaçao
15 ml/1 tablespoon lime juice
2 scoops lemon sorbet
Serves 1

Add all the ingredients to a blender. Blend for 20 seconds and pour into a margarita glass.

Starship Sandwiches

How enterprising! Beam your guests up with delight as you serve these star-shaped sarnies during *Star Trek*. Resistance is futile.

24 slices of bread, a mixture of brown and white, buttered
a selection of fillings of your choice such as cream cheese and tomato,
ham and mayonnaise, hoummus and sliced avocado
star-shaped pastry cutter
Serves 12

Arrange half the buttered bread slices on a work surface and top with a selection of fillings. Put the remaining bread slices on top and cut out shaped sandwiches with the star cutter.

Axiom Cookies

Munch on these bright, star-shaped cookies while watching WALL-E follow EVE into outer space to win her heart. If only he'd baked her some of these treats, she would most likely have fallen in love instantly. But then, robots aren't known for their baking skills.

215 g/15 tablespoons unsalted butter, softened

225 g/1 cup plus 2 tablespoons sugar

1 egg, beaten

½ teaspoon vanilla extract

a pinch of salt

440 g/3½ cups plain/all-purpose flour, sifted, plus extra for dusting

1 bag fruit-flavoured boiled sweets/hard candies

selection of shaped cookie cutters

2 baking sheets, lined with nonstick parchment paper

Makes about 24

Cream together the butter and sugar until light and creamy. Add the beaten egg, vanilla and salt and mix well. Gradually add the flour and mix until incorporated. Bring together into a dough, then flatten into a disc. Wrap in clingfilm/plastic wrap and refrigerate for 2 hours. Roll the dough out on a lightly floured work surface to a thickness of 3 mm/⅛ inch. Using the cookie cutters, carefully stamp out shapes. Arrange them on the prepared baking sheets. Using smaller cutters, cut out a shape in the middle of each cookie. Gather together the offcuts of the dough and re-roll to make more shapes. Refrigerate for 15 minutes. Preheat the oven to 180°C (350°F) Gas 4. Divide the boiled sweets/hard candies into separate colours and put them into plastic food bags. Using a rolling pin or pestle and mortar, crush the sweets/candies into small pieces. Take the sheets of cookies out of the fridge. Carefully fill the empty space in the middle of each biscuit with the crushed sweets/candies in an even, thin layer and no thicker than the depth of the cookies. Bake one sheet at a time on the middle shelf of the preheated oven for about 12 minutes or until the cookies are pale golden and the sweets/candies have melted to fill the space. Let the bcookies to cool on the baking sheets until the coloured centres have set.

Death Stars

In a kitchen far, far away, the recipe for peppermint creams was created. Many years have passed and now it's your duty to follow said recipe. While none will resemble the Death Star, each and every bite must be destroyed by your guests.

225 g/scant 2 cups icing/confectioners' sugar

4–6 tablespoons condensed milk

½ teaspoon peppermint extract

green food colouring paste (optional)

mini star-shaped cutter

Makes 20–30

Sift the icing/confectioners' sugar into a large bowl. Gradually add the condensed milk and peppermint extract, mixing with a wooden spoon. The mixture should come together like dough and you may need to use your hands towards the end of the mixing. To knead the dough, sprinkle a little icing/confectioners' sugar on a clean work surface. Shape the dough into a ball and push on it and press it onto the work surface, turning it round often. Do this for just a minute or so until smooth. If you like, you can divide the dough in half and tint one half green using a little of the food colouring. Knead the dough again until it is evenly green. On the work surface, roll the dough out using a rolling pin. Stamp out stars with your cookie cutter and arrange them on a sheet of parchment paper. Let the stars dry overnight before serving.

Giant Bug Pies

In a fight for survival, the Starship Troopers have to obliterate 'the Bugs', an extraterrestrial race that looks rather like a bunch of oversized grasshoppers. Demolishing these pies won't involve guns, trips to other planets or silly military tattoos, but eating them will be just as thrilling.

125 g/1 stick butter, softened
200 g/1 cup (caster) sugar
1 large egg
zest of 2 limes
320 g/2½ cups self-raising/
   self-rising flour
1 teaspoon baking powder
½ teaspoon salt
250 ml/1 cup buttermilk
100 ml/scant ½ cup hot water

Filling
4 leaves of gelatine
200 g/¾ cup cream cheese
300 ml/1¼ cups sour cream
200 g/1 cup (caster) sugar
freshly squeezed juice of 1
   orange and 1 lemon
juice and zest of 2 limes
green food colouring

Lime icing
200 g/1⅔ cups fondant
   icing/confectioners' sugar
2–3 tablespoons lime juice
a few drops green food colouring
50 mini lime jelly slices, chopped
two 12-hole whoopie pie pans, greased
piping bag fitted with a large star nozzle/tip
Makes 12

To make the filling, soak the gelatine leaves in cold water for 5 minutes. Put the cream cheese, sour cream and sugar in a blender and whizz until mixed. Put the juices and gelatine in a saucepan and heat gently until the gelatine has dissolved. Do not allow it to boil. Pour the citrus juices into the blender, add the lime zest and food colouring and mix again. Transfer to a bowl and set in the fridge for 2–3 hours. Preheat the oven to 180°C (350°F) Gas 4. Cream together the butter and sugar in a bowl for 2–3 minutes using a hand-held mixer until light and creamy. Add the egg and lime zest and mix again. Sift the flour and baking powder into

the bowl and add the salt and buttermilk. Whisk until incorporated. Whisk in the hot water. Put spoonfuls of mixture in the pans. Leave to stand for 10 minutes then bake for 10–12 minutes. Remove from the oven, let cool slightly then turn out to cool completely. To make the icing, mix together the icing/confectioners' sugar, lime juice and food colouring to form a smooth paste. Spread over 12 of the pie halves and top with the chopped lime jelly slices. Spoon the filling into a piping bag and pipe a swirl onto the un-iced pie halves. Top each with a decorated pie half and serve.

Intergalactic Cake

260 g/2¼ sticks unsalted
butter, softened
260 g/2¼ cups (caster)
sugar
1 teaspoon vanilla extract
4 eggs, lightly beaten
260 g/2 cups self-raising/
self-rising flour
¼ teaspoon baking
powder
1 tablespoon milk
red and green food
colouring
Chocolate ganache
200 g/7 oz. dark/
semisweet chocolate
250 ml/1 cup double/
heavy cream
25 g/2 tablespoons
unsalted butter
To decorate
100 g/3½ oz. chocolate,
grated
sprinkles and/or edible
silver balls
two 20-cm/8-inch round
cake pans, greased
Serves 8–10

No one was more surprised than Will Smith when aliens started attacking earth in *Independence Day*. Your guests' surprise when they tuck into this vivid cake may not be on the same level but they may exclaim, 'I have got to bake me one of these!'.

Preheat the oven to 180°C (350°F) Gas 4. Cream the butter and sugar together in a large bowl with a hand-held electric mixer until light and fluffy. Add the vanilla and beat in the eggs a little at a time. Sift in the flour and baking powder and fold in gently. If the mixture feels very stiff, add the milk to loosen it. Divide the mixture between 3 separate bowls. Add a few drops of food colouring to 2 of the bowls, leaving one untinted. Stir in the colourings gently until just combined. Put small dollops of the 3 mixtures in the prepared pans in a random pattern and then level the tops with a palette knife. Bake in the preheated oven for about 20–25 minutes, until a skewer inserted in the centre of the cake comes out clean. Let the cakes cool in the pans for a few minutes before turning out onto a wire rack to cool completely. To make the ganache, put the chocolate, cream and butter in a heavy-based saucepan and set over low heat. Stir gently until the chocolate melts into the cream. Take off the heat and let stand for a few minutes to cool and thicken slightly before using. Spread about 5 heaped tablespoons of the ganache over one half of the cooled cake and sandwich together with the other half. Working quickly, pour the rest of the ganache over the top of the cake and smooth it over the top and sides with a palette knife. Arrange the grated chocolate in the centre of the cake and add some sprinkles.

Space Shuttle

20-cm/8-inch round
   Madeira/pound cake,
   store-bought or
   homemade
450-g/16-oz. tub
   ready-made vanilla
   frosting
4 or 5 ready-made
   swiss/jelly rolls
6 ice cream cones
blue and red candies,
   silver balls and
   liquorice, to decorate
orange sugarpaste/
   fondant icing
Serves 8–10

Grab your tissues and a slice of this spacey cake as you watch E.T. and Elliot wish each other a tearful farewell right before the cute alien steps on board his spaceship to head home. Sob (and yum).

Trim the crust from the Madeira/pound cake and slice the top flat. This will create the base of the spaceship. Using a little of the frosting, stick together the swiss/jelly rolls. This will form the middle part of the ship. Place them on top of the base, then stick an upturned ice-cream cone on top of them to form the pointed tip of the spaceship. Cover the whole cake with the remaining frosting. Put the cake on a round cake board and stick five ice-cream cones around the base to form the space shuttle 'legs'. Decorate the spaceship using blue and red candies, silver balls and liquorice wheels for portholes. Roll out the orange sugarpaste/fondant icing and cut into little triangles. Stick these around the base of the rocket and up around the sides to create a flame effect.

KEIRA KNIGHTLEY

JOHNNY DEPP · GEOFFREY RUSH · ORLANDO BLOOM

PIRATES *of the* **CARIBBEAN**
THE CURSE OF THE BLACK PEARL

LARA CROFT TOMB RAIDER

IN THEATRES JUNE 15
TOMBRAIDERMOVIE.COM

Action-Adventure

'Out in the garage, O... ORV, four-wheel drive, bullet holes the size of matzah balls!' — The Goonies

Action-adventure films are often shot in exotic locations. While transforming your living room into a desert or jungle would prove challenging, you could use props to give the illusion of a land far flung. Some stuffed camels, fake scorpions and scattered sand (so long as you're OK with vacuuming up afterwards) would do the job for a desert scene. If you're feeling adventurous, you could even perform a belly dance for your enraptured/amused guests. Or if a jungle setting is more appropriate, how about some cuddly monkeys, fake snakes and strewn greenery? In terms of costumes, this genre provides many options – pirates, explorers, gunfighters, treasure-seekers, or more specific characters such as Indiana Jones and Lara Croft. If you're screening two or more films, a fun game you could play during 'intermission' is the 'mummy game', which involves teaming up and wrapping your partner in toilet paper until they resemble an Egyptian mummy. It'll get people moving, giggling and excited for the next swashbuckling/rope-swinging/hat-retrieving adventure. Or, if you want to make your guests work for their food, you could hand out a treasure map that takes them on a hunt around your house and garden in search of the 'hidden treasure' (food).

IT'S SHOWTIME!

Indiana Jones, Smokey and the Bandit, Mad Max, Cars, Around the World in 80 Days, Treasure Island, The Mask Of Zorro, Lara Croft: Tomb Raider, The Goonies, Pirates of the Caribbean, Gulliver's Travels, Robin Hood: Prince of Thieves, The Mummy, Hook, Harry Potter, Puss in Boots, The Three Musketeers, Lord of the Rings, Brave, Honey, I Shrunk the Kids, Labyrinth, Tarzan, Romancing the Stone, Bill & Ted's Excellent Adventure.

Peanut Butter Popcorn

It seems only fitting to watch the antics of a 'nutty' character while eating peanut butter popcorn. It doesn't get much nuttier than the scientist Wayne Szalinski in *Honey, I Shrunk The Kids*, who had to explain to his wife that their children were now the size of insects thanks to one of his wacky inventions.

1–2 tablespoons sunflower or vegetable oil

90 g/⅓ cup popcorn kernels

170 g/¼ cup peanut butter (smooth or crunchy)

80 g/5½ tablespoons butter

50 g/¼ cup sugar

1 teaspoon vanilla extract

100 g/¾ cup honey roasted peanuts

Makes 1 large bowl

Heat the oil in a large lidded saucepan with a few popcorn kernels in the pan. When you hear the kernels pop, carefully tip in the rest of the kernels. Shake the pan over the heat until the popping stops. Take care when lifting the lid as any unpopped kernels may pop from the heat of the pan. Tip the popcorn into a bowl, removing any unpopped kernels as you go. Put the peanut butter, butter, sugar and vanilla extract in a small saucepan and heat until the butter has melted and the sugar has dissolved, stirring all the time so the sauce does not stick. Pour the peanut butter sauce over the popcorn and stir well so that the popcorn is evenly coated. Tip in the peanuts and stir again to mix through. Serve warm or cold.

Paradise Island Punch

**500 ml/2 cups dark
Jamaican rum**
**100 ml/½ cup Wray and
Nephew overproof rum**
**250 ml/1 cup fresh lime
juice (about 8 limes)**
**100 ml/⅓ cup orgeat
syrup**
**500 ml/2 cups passion
fruit juice**
**500 ml/2 cups pineapple
juice**
**fresh fruit and fresh mint
sprigs, to garnish**
Serves 10

The tropical Thai island of Koh Phi Phi is where *The Beach* was set, a flick that packs some serious punch. Sip away as you witness Richard (Leonardo DiCaprio) get consumed by paradise.

Add all the ingredients to a large pitcher or punch bowl filled with ice and stir gently to mix. Serve in ice-filled glasses garnished with seasonal fruit and fresh mint sprigs.

Hannibal's Jalapeño Poppers

20 Jalapeño chillies/chiles
140 g/1¼ cups grated
**   mature/sharp Cheddar**
50 g/⅓ cup plain/
**   all-purpose flour**
1 egg beaten
vegetable oil, for deep-frying
Serves 8-10

Hailing from Mexico, which is where leader of *The A-Team*, Hannibal, was held captive, the spicy jalapeño is the perfect garnish to a night of explosions, mudsuckers and cigar chewing. Don't you just love it when a dish comes together?

Slit the jalapeños along one side and carefully remove the seeds then stuff generously with the grated cheese. Roll the jalapeños in the flour, dip in the beaten egg and coat once more with flour ensuring that they are completely covered in flour. Heat the oil to 190°C (375°F) – if you don't have a thermometer, the oil is ready when a 2.5-cm/1-inch cube of white bread dropped into the oil browns in approximately 60 seconds. Fry the chillies/chiles in small batches for 6–7 minutes until golden brown. Remove them from the pan using a slotted spoon, drain off the excess oil and serve.

Spicy Sausage Chilli

Appreciate a spicy Spanish sausage as you watch the sizzling Spanish actor Antonio Banderas in *The Mask Of Zorro*. Like this meal, his sexy accent, sword-fighting panache and ability to de-robe Catherine Zeta-Jones is nothing short of hot, hot, hot.

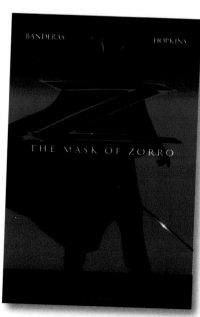

250 g/9 oz. chorizo, finely chopped
2–3 tablespoons vegetable oil
1 large onion, diced
4 mixed (bell) peppers, diced
2 celery stalks, with leaves, diced
2 teaspoons dried red chilli/hot pepper flakes
½ teaspoon cayenne pepper
2½ teaspoons ground cumin
2 teaspoons dried oregano
2 garlic cloves, finely chopped
250 g/9 oz. minced/ground beef
250 ml/1 cup red wine

500 ml/2 cups beef
   stock or water
1 bay leaf
400-g/14-oz. can
   chopped tomatoes
2 x 400-g/14-oz cans black beans, drained
a handful of fresh coriander/cilantro leaves,
   chopped
fresh red chillies/chiles, sliced and deseeded
sea salt
sour cream or crème fraîche, to serve

Serves 4

Put the chorizo in a small saucepan and set over medium heat. Cook until browned then transfer to a plate lined with kitchen paper/paper towels and set aside. Heat 2 tablespoons of the oil in a large saucepan. Add the onion and cook for 2–3 minutes until soft. Add the peppers and celery, season with a little salt, and cook for a further 3–5 minutes, until soft. Stir in the chilli/hot pepper flakes, cayenne pepper, cumin, oregano and garlic and cook, stirring, for 1 minute. Add the beef and cook for 5–7 minutes, stirring occasionally, until browned. Season with a little more salt. Add the wine and cook for 1 minute, then stir in the stock, bay leaf, tomatoes and beans. Cover, reduce the heat and simmer for 15 minutes. Taste the seasoning and adjust as necessary. Continue simmering, uncovered, for a further 20–30 minutes. When ready to serve, stir in the coriander/cilantro. Scatter over the fresh chillies/chiles and serve the sour cream on the side.

Temple of Doom Cookies

Watch *Indiana Jones and the Temple Of Doom* and, just when Willie is being served eyeball soup, offer your guests an eyeball cookie. If they are horrified, simply say, 'Hey, at least it's not chilled monkey brains or snake surprise.'

100 g/7 tablespoons unsalted butter, softened
50 g/3 tablespoons crunchy peanut butter
100 g/½ cup (caster) sugar
1 large egg yolk
1 teaspoon vanilla extract
150 g/1 cup plus 3 tablespoons plain/all-purpose flour
a pinch of salt

To decorate
50 g/2 oz. sugarpaste/fondant icing
green, blue and red food colouring
300 g/10½ oz. white chocolate
24 brown candy-coated chocolate drops
baking sheet, lined with nonstick parchment paper
cocktail sticks/toothpicks
Makes about 24

Preheat the oven to 180˚C (350˚F) Gas 4. Put the butter, peanut butter and sugar in a mixing bowl and cream until pale and light. Add the egg yolk and vanilla extract and mix until combined. Tip the flour and salt into the bowl and mix again until smooth. Pull off walnut-sized pieces of dough and roll into balls between your hands. Arrange on the prepared baking sheet. Press your finger into the top of each cookie to make an indent. Bake the cookies on the middle shelf of the oven for about 12 minutes until golden and firm. Let cool on the baking sheet for 2–3 minutes before transferring to a wire rack until cold. To decorate, divide the icing in half and put each portion in its own bowl. Tint one portion green and one blue using the food colouring. Divide the blue icing into 12 equal portions, roll into balls and flatten into discs. Repeat with the green icing. Cover them all with clingfilm/plastic wrap and set aside. Melt the white chocolate in a heatproof bowl over a pan of barely simmering water. Do not let the base of the bowl touch the water. Stir until smooth, then let cool and thicken slightly. Taking one cookie at a time, dip it into the melted chocolate and place on a wire rack. Position either a blue or green icing disc in the dent in the middle of the cookie. Dip one side of a chocolate drop in the melted chocolate, then position on the icing disc. Dip a toothpick/cocktail stick into the red food colouring paste and wiggle red, veiny lines across the white chocolate. Allow to set before serving.

Gingerbread Pirates

He may not have the long-locked good looks of Captain Jack Sparrow (Johnny Depp), but he's just as yummy. Chomp on this buccaneer cookie while watching any one of the *Pirates of the Caribbean* films, matey. Arrr!

450 g/1 lb. ready-made gingerbread cookie dough
500 g/1 lb 2oz. royal icing mix
75–100 ml/⅓–½ cup water
black, red, yellow and blue food colourings
6 small yellow sugar-coated chocolate drops

gingerbread-man cutter
baking sheets, lined
with nonstick parchment paper
4 piping bags with small, round nozzles/tips
Makes about 6

Preheat the oven to 170°C (325°F) Gas 3. Roll out the dough on a clean work surface lightly dusted with flour. Stamp out as many cookies as possible with the cutter and arrange the cookies on the prepared baking sheets. Cut one of the legs on each man into a stump shape. Bake in batches on the middle shelf of the oven for 10–12 minutes or until firm and lightly browned. Let the cookies cool completely before icing. Put the royal icing mix in a bowl and add the water gradually to form a thick, smooth paste. Leave 1 teaspoon of the icing in the mixing bowl, cover and set aside. Spoon one quarter of the remaining icing into a bowl and tint it black using food colouring. Divide the remaining icing between 3 bowls and tint one bowl red, one yellow and one blue.

Spoon 2 tablespoons of the blue icing into the piping bag and pipe an outline for the pirates' trousers and headscarf. Use the yellow icing to draw an outline for his t-shirt. Use the black icing to draw outlines for the boots and the peg leg. Let dry. Flood the trousers and headscarf sections with the blue icing. Pipe red and yellow stripes across the t-shirt. Flood the boots and peg leg with black icing. Let dry. Pipe black icing across the pirates' waists to make a belt and put a yellow chocolate drop in the middle as a buckle. Give each pirate a black eye patch and pipe yellow polka dots onto the headscarf, plus a yellow button on the boot. Pipe a dot of white and black icing for the eyes and give each pirate a red grin. Let dry completely before serving.

Mummified Cupcakes

Frightfully delicious, the adventure-horror movie *The Mummy* would complement these cupcakes amazingly. Make a second batch so that when your guests have polished them off you can bring more out and declare, '*The Mummy Returns!*' while popping the sequel into the DVD player.

225 g/2 sticks unsalted
    butter, softened
225 g/1 cup plus 2
    tablespoons (caster)
    sugar
4 large eggs, beaten
1 teaspoon vanilla extract
225 g/1¾ cups self-raising/
    self-rising flour
2 tablespoons milk
Meringue buttercream
200 g/1 cup (caster) sugar
3 egg whites
250 g/2 sticks unsalted
    butter, softened and
    diced
1 teaspoon vanilla extract
24 edible sugar eyes
12-hole muffin pan, lined
with muffin cases
piping bag, fitted with a
1-cm/⅜-inch flat-sided
nozzle/tip
Makes 12

Preheat the oven to 180°C (350°F) Gas 4. Cream the butter and sugar until pale and light in a free-standing electric mixer. Gradually add the beaten eggs and vanilla extract, mixing well between each addition. Sift the flour into the bowl and mix until thoroughly combined and smooth. Add the milk and mix again. Divide the batter between the muffin cases and bake the cupcakes on the middle shelf of the preheated oven for 20–25 minutes or until golden, well risen and a wooden skewer inserted into the middle of the cakes comes out clean. Cool the cakes in the pans for 3–4 minutes and then transfer to a wire rack until cool. To make the buttercream, put the sugar and egg whites in a heatproof bowl set over a pan of simmering water and whisk until the sugar has dissolved and the mixture starts to thicken and turn white. Remove from the heat, scoop the meringue into the electric mixer and whisk on medium speed for another 3 minutes until very thick and glossy white. Gradually add the diced butter to the cold meringue mix, beating constantly until the frosting is smooth. Add the vanilla extract. Spoon the frosting into the piping bag and pipe bands criss-crossing each other across the top of each cake, almost covering the cake completely but leaving a little space for the eyes. Press 2 sugar eyes into the frosting on each cake to serve.

Hot-Air Balloon Cake

Phileas Fogg embarked on quite the challenge when he declared that he could travel around the world in 80 days, beginning his journey in a hot-air balloon. While you follow his escapades, encourage guests to see if this cake can go 'around the room in 80 bites'.

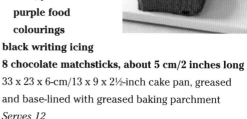

350 g/3 sticks unsalted butter, softened
350 g/1¾ cups (caster) sugar
6 large eggs, beaten
2 teaspoons vanilla extract
350 g/2¾ cups plain/all-purpose flour
5 teaspoons baking powder
4–5 tablespoons milk, at room temperature
Buttercream
350 g/3 sticks unsalted butter, softened
700 g/5¾ cups icing/confectioners' sugar, sifted

brown, red, green,
   blue, yellow and
   purple food
   colourings
black writing icing
8 chocolate matchsticks, about 5 cm/2 inches long
33 x 23 x 6-cm/13 x 9 x 2½-inch cake pan, greased
and base-lined with greased baking parchment
Serves 12

Preheat the oven to 180°C (350°F) Gas 4. Cream the butter and sugar in a free-standing electric mixer until pale and light. Gradually add the beaten eggs, mixing well between each addition. Stir in the vanilla. Sift together the flour and baking powder and add to the cake batter, mixing until smooth. Add the milk and mix until smooth. Spoon into the prepared cake pan. Bake on the middle shelf of the preheated oven for 45 minutes or until a skewer inserted into the middle of the cake comes out clean. Let the cake cool in the pan for 10 minutes before turning out on to a wire rack. Cream the butter and icing/confectioners' sugar in the mixer until pale and smooth. Put 3–4 tablespoons of the buttercream in a

bowl and tint it brown. Divide the remaining buttercream between 5 bowls and tint each one a different colour. Draw a balloon shape on a piece of paper. Cut out the template and lay it on top of the cake, then cut around it with a sharp knife. Cut off the 2 leftover corners of the cake in equal triangles and stick together with buttercream to make a square basket shape. Spread the coloured buttercreams in stripes over the balloon. Pipe lines between the stripes with black writing icing. Push the chocolate matchsticks into the underside of the balloon. Position the basket below the balloon and cover with brown buttercream, making a weave effect with a fork. Push the basket against the matchsticks carefully.

CAPTAIN AMERICA

Fighting for the
American Dream!

Comic Book Heroes

'This will be a piece of cake. Or, even better, a slice of pizza!' –
Teenage Mutant Ninja Turtles

Holy superhero movie night, Batman! Kids and adults alike will definitely get a kick out of this theme. You can really go to town (or Gotham City) when decorating. Either buy some comic book wrapping paper or print individual comic book covers from the internet and plaster them around your lounge – interspersed with signs saying 'POW! BOOM! BAM! KAPOW!' and superhero logos like the Batman symbol and the Superman 'S'. Pin streamers across the room and, using fishing line or cotton, hang different superheroes along them, as though they are poised and ready to jump in on the action at any second. Ask guests to dress up as their favourite superhero or comic book villain. To stand out as the host cooking up a storm, you could wear a superhero apron. In case anyone forgets to dress up, have a mask or two spare so they don't feel left out among the other caped crusaders. Or you could hand out fake superhero tattoos for them to wear. During the evening, pose this question: 'If you could have one superpower, what would it be and why?' The answers may be quite illuminating! Perhaps someone will opt for invisibility so they can eat your entire superhero spread without anyone suspecting it was them!

IT'S SHOWTIME!

The Incredible Hulk, The Avengers, Iron Man, Captain America, Batman, Spider-Man, Popeye, G.I. Joe: Retaliation, Superman, X-Men, The Incredibles, Thor, Kick-Ass, Supergirl, Teenage Mutant Ninja Turtles, The Shadow, Judge Dredd, Tank Girl, Mighty Morphin Power Rangers: The Movie, Transformers, The Phantom, Unbreakable, Daredevil, Hancock, The Green Hornet.

Captain America Popcorn

Patriotic popcorn for the ultimate patriotic superhero. Depending on how much flag-waving world-saving you can take, you could settle in to watch an array of *Captain America* movies — the original from 1944, the update from 1990 and the bicep-bulging version from 2011.

1–2 tablespoons sunflower or vegetable oil
90 g/⅓ cup popcorn kernels
80 g/5½ tablespoons butter
red and blue food colourings
60 g/5 tablespoons sugar
Makes 1 large bowl

Heat the oil in a large lidded saucepan with a few popcorn kernels in the pan. When you hear the kernels pop, carefully tip in the rest of the kernels. Shake the pan over the heat until the popping stops. Take care when lifting the lid, as any unpopped kernels may still pop from the heat of the pan. Divide the popcorn into 3 bowls, removing any unpopped kernels as you go. Divide the butter between 2 small saucepans and heat gently until melted. Add a few drops of red food colouring to one pan and a few drops of blue to the other and stir. Pour the red butter over one of the bowls of popcorn and stir well so that the popcorn is evenly coated. Do the same with the blue butter. The third bowl remains white. Leave the popcorn to set for about 20 minutes (or the colours will run together). After this time, add all the popcorn to a bowl, sprinkle with the sugar and stir to mix. Serve in the bowl or divide between bags and seal with pretty, matching ribbon. This popcorn can be served warm or cold, but if you are sealing in bags, make sure the popcorn is cold before you do so.

Matt Salinger is...

CAPTAIN AMERICA

Fighting for the American Dream!

The Hulk's Smash

Have you invited a guest with a fiery temper? Hopefully this green cocktail won't rile them up as you all watch the *The Incredible Hulk* declare, 'You're making me angry. You wouldn't like me when I'm angry.'

25 ml/1 oz. tequila
25 ml/1 oz. Midori
25 ml/1 oz. lime juice
25 ml/1 oz. Cointreau
Serves 1

Add the all ingredients to a shaker filled with ice. Shake sharply and strain into a rocks glass.

Popeye Pie

Before *Popeye the Sailor Man* hit the big screen, he was on the small screen...
and before that, he was a beloved comic-book character. One trait that's never
changed about him is that his strength is boosted by spinach. Enhance your
guests' muscles with these egg and spinach pies as they watch Popeye woo
Olive Oyl and tussle with Bluto.

2 tablespoons extra
    virgin olive oil, plus
    extra to glaze
1 small onion, finely
    chopped
225 g/8 oz. fresh spinach
250 g/1 cup ricotta
4 tablespoons freshly
    grated Parmesan
75 g/2½ cups rocket/
    arugula, finely
    chopped
1 teaspoon freshly
    chopped tarragon
freshly grated nutmeg
450 g/1 lb ready-made
    shortcrust pastry
8 eggs
sea salt and freshly
    ground black pepper
large, heavy baking sheet
round cookie cutter
two 4-hole muffin pans
Makes 8 pies

Preheat the oven to 220°C (425°F) Gas 7. Put the baking sheet in the oven to
heat for at least 30 minutes. Heat the olive oil in a frying pan, add the onion
and fry for 5 minutes until golden. Let cool. Steam the spinach until just
wilted, refresh in cold water, then squeeze out as much moisture as possible
and roughly chop. Beat the spinach and onion into the ricotta with the
Parmesan, rocket/arugula and tarragon. Season well with salt, pepper and
nutmeg. Roll out the pastry on a clean, lightly floured work surface. Cut out
8 circles with the cutter. Use these to line
each muffin cup. Fill each pie with some of
the ricotta mixture. Make a small indent in
each filling. Break the eggs one at a time,
separating the yolks from the whites. Slip a
yolk into the indent of each pie. Season
with salt and pepper. Roll the pastry
offcuts into long, thin ropes and cut into
16 lengths. Use these to make a cross on
top of each pie, sealing the edges with a
little water. Brush lightly with olive oil.
Bake in the oven for 10 minutes until the
egg is just set and the pastry cooked.
Serve hot.

The Rock Cakes

Get the night rocking with these deliciously dense cakes and *G.I. Joe: Retaliation*, which sees many a tough guy – including Dwayne 'The Rock' Johnson – getting sweaty and saving the world.

250 g/2 cups plain/all-purpose flour

2 teaspoons baking powder

30 g/2½ tablespoons salted butter, diced

30 g/2½ tablespoons white vegetable shortening

50 g/⅓ cup mixed candied peel, finely chopped

60 g/⅓ cup (caster) sugar

50 g/⅓ cup sultanas/golden raisins

50 g/⅓ cup currants

2 eggs

5 tablespoons milk

1 tablespoon light brown sugar

baking sheet lined with nonstick parchment paper

Makes 12

Preheat the oven to 200°C (400°F) Gas 6. Sift the flour and baking powder into a large bowl. Add the butter and vegetable shortening, add to the bowl and rub together using your fingertips to a fine crumb texture. Add the sugar and dried fruit and stir together. In a separate bowl, lightly beat the eggs and milk together, then add to the flour mixture and blend to a firm-ish dough. The mixture should be soft but not sticky or dry. Add a splash more milk, if needed. Using 2 dessertspoons, shape the mixture into 12 rough mounds on the prepared baking sheet. Sprinkle the brown sugar over the top. Bake in the middle of the preheated oven for 15 minutes or until the edges of the cakes turn a pale golden brown colour. Transfer the cakes to a wire rack to cool.

Spider Cookies

While Spider-Man had to remind himself that 'with great power comes great responsibility', you should be proud that 'with great parties come great recipes'. These eight-legged cuties will get your guests' spider-senses tingling for sure — not to mention their taste buds.

125 g/1 stick unsalted butter, softened
225 g/1 cup plus 2 tablespoons (caster) sugar
1 egg, lightly beaten
1 teaspoon vanilla extract
175 g/1⅓ cups plain/ all-purpose flour
50 g/⅓ cup unsweetened cocoa powder
½ teaspoon baking powder
½ teaspoon bicarbonate of soda/baking soda
a pinch of salt
3 tablespoons sugar

Filling
100 g/6½ tablespoons unsalted butter
150 g/1¼ cups icing/confectioners' sugar
1 teaspoon vanilla extract
green and orange food colouring
48 green and orange candy-coated chocolate drops and black liquorice strips, to decorate
baking sheets, lined with nonstick baking parchment
piping bag, fitted with a round nozzle/tip
Makes about 24

Preheat the oven to 180°C (350°F) Gas 4. Put the butter and sugar in a mixing bowl and cream until pale and light. Add the beaten egg and vanilla extract and mix until combined. Sift the flour, cocoa, baking powder, bicarbonate of soda/baking soda and salt into the mixing bowl and mix again until smooth. Pull off pieces of dough about the size of large marbles and roll into balls between your hands. Press the top of each cookie into the granulated sugar and arrange on the prepared baking sheets, then slightly flatten each one with your fingers. Bake on the middle shelf of the preheated oven for no more than 12 minutes – do not overbake otherwise they will become bitter. Let cool on the baking sheets. To make the buttercream filling, put the butter, sugar and vanilla extract in a mixing bowl and cream until pale and light. Remove 2 tablespoons of buttercream and set aside. Divide the remaining buttercream in half and tint one portion green and one portion orange using the food colourings. Spread orange buttercream over the underside of 12 of the cookies and the green buttercream over the underside of another 12. Top with the remaining cookies. Spoon the untinted buttercream into the piping bag and pipe 2 eyes on top of each spider. Cut the liquorice strips into small spider-leg lengths – you will need 8 for each cookie. Press the chocolate drops onto the buttercream eyes and push the 8 licorice legs into the sides of each cookie to serve.

Black Widow's Bite

Get a double-whammy of the Black Widow femme fatale, played by Scarlett Johansson, in *The Avengers* and *Iron Man 2*. Watch her weave her web of destruction and kick some serious butt while you and your guests relax with a cobweb cupcake.

115 g/½ cup plus 1 tablespoon light brown sugar

125 ml/1½ cup sunflower oil

2 eggs

115 g/1 cup grated pumpkin or butternut squash flesh

grated zest of 1 lemon

115 g/1 cup self-raising/ self-rising flour

1 teaspoon baking powder

1 teaspoon ground cinnamon

To decorate

150 g/5½ oz. white chocolate, chopped

25 g/1 oz. dark/ semisweet chocolate

12-hole cupcake pan, lined with cake cases

piping bag fitted with a round nozzle/tip

Makes 12

Preheat the oven to 180°C (350°F) Gas 4. Put the sugar in a bowl and break up with the back of a fork, then beat in the oil and eggs. Fold in the grated pumpkin and lemon zest. Combine the flour, baking powder and cinnamon in a bowl, then sift into the mixture and fold in. Spoon the mixture into the paper cases and bake in the preheated oven for about 18 minutes until risen and a skewer inserted in the middle comes out clean. Transfer to a wire rack to cool.

To decorate, put the white and dark/semisweet chocolates in separate heatproof bowls set over pans of gently simmering water. Do not let the bases of the bowls touch the water. Leave until almost melted. Remove from the heat and let cool for about 5 minutes, then spoon the white chocolate over the cakes. Spoon the dark/semisweet chocolate into the piping bag and snip the tip off so that you can pipe a thin line of chocolate. Put a dot of chocolate in the middle of each cake, then pipe 3 concentric circles around the dot. Using a skewer, draw a line from the central dot to the outside edge of the cake and repeat about 8 times all the way round to create a spider's web pattern. Serve while the chocolate is still slightly soft and gooey.

Kryptonite Panna Cotta

1½ tablespoons matcha
    green tea powder
6 tablespoons milk
2 teaspoons powdered
    gelatine
500 ml/2 cups
    double/heavy cream
70 g/⅓ cup sugar
four 140-g/5-oz. teacups or
dariole moulds
Serves 4

Kryptonite is Superman's one weakness (other than Lois Lane, of course) and resembles this green dessert. After a couple of mouthfuls, it's possible that you'll have found one of your biggest weaknesses too.

Gradually mix the matcha green tea powder with 1–2 tablespoons of the milk in a small bowl until smooth. Pour the remaining milk into a small heatproof bowl and sprinkle over the gelatine. Set aside for about 5 minutes, then place the bowl over a shallow saucepan of hot water and stir until dissolved. Let cool. Put the cream and sugar in a saucepan and set over low heat until almost boiling. Remove from the heat and pour into a large glass measuring cup. Beat in the matcha powder mixture, then the gelatine solution. Beat until fully blended. Pour the mixture into the teacups or dariole moulds. Refrigerate for 1–2 hours until set. The panna cottas should wobble but they shouldn't look as though they are liquid in the middle. If you've made the panna cottas in dariole moulds, dip the bases briefly in boiling water, then invert onto plates and give one short, sharp shake to loosen them. They should drop out easily. If you've made them in teacups, serve as they are.

Bat Cake

The coolest thing to come out of the Bat Cave since the Bat Mobile, if the caped crusader served the Joker, the Penguin or Catwoman a slice of this nom-nom-nocturnal cake, he'd have his rivals eating out of the palm of his wing. To the kitchen, Robin!

300 g/2⅓ cups plain/all-purpose flour

2 rounded tablespoons unsweetened cocoa powder

1 teaspoon baking powder

2 teaspoons bicarbonate of soda/baking soda

a pinch of salt

200 g/14 tablespoons unsalted butter, softened

325 g/1⅔ cups (caster) sugar

1 teaspoon vanilla extract

4 large eggs, beaten

125 g/4½ oz. dark/semisweet chocolate, melted

225 ml/1 cup sour cream, at room temperature

175 ml/⅔ cup boiling water

1 quantity buttercream (page 97)

500 g/1 lb. blue sugarpaste or fondant icing

250 g/8 oz. black sugarpaste or fondant icing

icing/confectioners' sugar, for dusting

edible sugar eyes

two 23-cm/9-inch cake pans, greased and baselined with greased nonstick parchment paper

Serves 8–10

Preheat the oven to 180°C (350°F) Gas 4. Sift together the first 5 ingredients. Cream together the butter, sugar and vanilla extract in a free-standing electric mixer until pale and light. Gradually add the beaten eggs, mixing well between each addition. Add the melted chocolate and mix until combined. Add one third of the dry ingredients and mix until combined and then add one third of the sour cream. Continue to add alternate batches of flour and sour cream. Add the boiling water and mix again until smooth. Divide the mixture between the prepared cake pans and bake on the middle shelf of the preheated oven for around 25 minutes or until well risen and a wooden skewer inserted into the middle of the cakes comes out clean. Cool the cakes in the pans for 3 minutes, then turn out onto wire racks until cold. Spread the top of one of the cakes with buttercream. Top with the second cake layer, gently pressing the 2 cakes together. Cover the sides and top of the cake in a smooth, even layer of buttercream. Chill in the fridge for 20 minutes. Roll out the blue icing into a disc large enough to completely cover the top and sides of the cake. Roll the icing around the rolling pin and then carefully unroll it over the cake, covering the top and sides. Trim off any excess. Roll out the black icing and cut out a large bat shape with a sharp knife. Brush the middle of the top of the cake with water and fix the bat on top. Cut out smaller bats and stick these to the sides and/or top of the cake with water. Add sugar eyes to the bats and serve.

James Bond

'Peking duck is different from Russian caviar. But I love them both' — *You Only Live Twice*

In your opinion, who's the best Bond? Sean Connery? George Lazenby? Roger Moore? Timothy Dalton? Pierce Brosnan? Daniel Craig? Whoever it is, a 007 movie night is the perfect way to relive those famous Bond moments while feasting on sophisticated fare suitably fit for this suave spy. If you're sending out invitations, mark them 'top secret' and ask guests to accept an undercover-mission briefing at the time and location of the party. State that the dress code is strictly black tie and evening gown – or, alternatively, encourage guests to dress as a specific character like villainous henchman Oddjob or sexy Bond girl Pussy Galore. To decorate, you could pin up Bond movie posters and place model Aston Martin cars around the room. To test guests' Bond knowledge, split them into three teams – Bond girls, spies and villains – and pose trivia questions for them to answer. Or set up a 'casino' with a poker table and roulette wheel, providing your guests with chips they can bet with. The winner at the end of the night could be rewarded with a James Bond box set. Play the soundtrack to the films in the background and set up a martini bar in the corner of the room.

IT'S SHOWTIME!

Dr. No, From Russia with Love, Goldfinger, Thunderball, You Only Live Twice, On Her Majesty's Secret Service, Diamonds Are Forever, Never Say Never Again, Live and Let Die, The Man with the Golden Gun, The Spy Who Loved Me, Moonraker, For Your Eyes Only, Octopussy, A View to a Kill, The Living Daylights, Licence to Kill, GoldenEye, Tomorrow Never Dies, The World Is Not Enough, Die Another Day, Casino Royale, Quantum of Solace, Skyfall.

Coconut Popcorn

There's no shortage of tropical locations in Bond films, but if you want to cater to both your male and female guests' desires, screen *Die Another Day* so the guys can drool over Halle Berry sashaying out of the sea, and *Casino Royale* so the ladies can get all hot and bothered over Daniel Craig doing the same.

100 g/1 cup long soft shredded coconut
1–2 tablespoons sunflower or vegetable oil
90 g/⅓ cup popcorn kernels
100 g/7 tablespoons extra virgin coconut oil
60 g/⅓ cup (caster) sugar
Makes 1 large bowl

In a small heavy-based frying pan, dry roast the shredded coconut, stirring constantly, until it starts to colour and give off a nutty aroma. It is important to keep moving it around the pan, as coconut can burn very easily. Remove from the pan, tip onto a plate and set aside. Heat the oil in a large lidded saucepan with a few popcorn kernels in the pan. When you hear the kernels pop, carefully tip in the rest of the kernels. Shake the pan over the heat until the popping stops. Take care when lifting the lid, as any unpopped kernels may still pop from the heat of the pan. Tip the popcorn into a bowl, removing any unpopped kernels as you go. Put the coconut oil in a small saucepan and heat gently, stirring, until it has melted. Pour the melted coconut oil over the popcorn, sprinkle over the toasted coconut and sugar and stir well until all the popcorn is evenly coated. This popcorn can be served warm or cold.

007 Martini

You've probably heard this one... A man walks into a bar and orders a vodka martini, shaken not stirred. But this isn't just any man; this is Bond, James Bond, whose sophisticated tipple of choice has become as synonymous with his character as always getting the girl.

a dash of vermouth
60 ml/2 oz. well-chilled gin or vodka
olive or lemon twist, to garnish
Serves 1

Add both the ingredients to a mixing glass filled with ice and shake. Strain into a chilled martini glass and garnish with an olive or lemon twist.

Crab Key Toasts

1 baguette
500 g/1 lb. 2 oz. fresh
   lump crabmeat
200 g/7 oz. fromage frais
Salsa
200 g/7 oz. radishes,
   roughly chopped
70 g/⅓ cup capers,
   drained and chopped
40 g/½ cup snipped fresh
   chives
4 tablespoons olive oil
4 tablespoons ginger
   wine
Makes 40

Owned by evil Dr. No, the private island of Crab Key housed an underground lair, which Bond had to escape, but not before witnessing one of the most famous scenes in film history – Honey Rider emerging from the ocean in a beautiful white bikini. Enjoy these crab and fromage frais toasts while witnessing the same spectacle.

Preheat the oven to 200°C (400°F) Gas 6. Slice the bread into 40 even slices and bake on baking sheets in the oven for about 10 minutes until nicely browned. Gently combine the fresh crabmeat and fromage frais in a bowl and chill in the fridge. When you are ready to serve, mix all the salsa ingredients together in a separate bowl. Use a small palette knife to spread the cold crab mixture onto the toasts, then top with a little salsa. Serve immediately.

Saucy Asparagus

Hollandaise sauce originated in France, just like the Bond girls from the following films: *Moonraker*, *For Your Eyes Only*, *The World Is Not Enough*, *Casino Royale* and *Skyfall*. Bon appétit!

150 g/1⅓ sticks unsalted butter
2 tablespoons white wine vinegar
1 shallot, finely chopped
a pinch of sea salt
2 egg yolks
asparagus spears, to serve
Serves 2

Melt the butter very gently in a small saucepan. Pour it into a small jug/pitcher through a muslin-lined tea strainer to remove any excess milk solids. Put the vinegar, shallot, salt and 1 tablespoon water in a small saucepan and heat gently until the liquid is almost totally evaporated, leaving only about 1 tablespoon. Remove from the heat and strain into a glass bowl. Put the bowl over a saucepan of barely simmering water. Do not let the base of the bowl touch the water. Add the egg yolks and, using a balloon whisk, whisk the mixture for 2 minutes, or until pale and frothy. Remove from the heat. Using a hand-held electric whisk, whisk in the melted butter, pouring it in in a slow, steady stream. Continue whisking until the sauce becomes thick and velvety. Serve warm.

Russian Roast Potatoes

24 small new potatoes, halved

3 tablespoons olive oil

200 ml/¾ cup crème fraîche/sour cream

125 ml/4½ oz. caviar

3 tablespoons snipped chives

sea salt and freshly ground black pepper

Serves 4–6

Caviar is seen as quintessentially Russian, so watching a movie with Russian characters would fit well here. There are many to choose from – Agent XXX in *The Spy Who Loved Me*, Natalya Simonova in *GoldenEye* and General Orlov in *Octopussy*, to name but a few. Bond also mentions this high-living delicacy in a number of films, including *Thunderball, On Her Majesty's Secret Service* and *A View to a Kill*.

Preheat the oven to 200ºC (400ºF) Gas 6. Place the potatoes on a large baking sheet and drizzle with the olive oil. Season well with salt and pepper. Bake them uncovered, in the preheated oven for 40 minutes, until crisp. Serve the potatoes warm, arranged on a plate with small bowls of the caviar, crème fraîche/sour cream and chives on the side.

Goldfinger Wraps with Guacamole

3 tablespoons mayonnaise
few drops Tabasco sauce
1 teaspoon sun-dried
   tomato paste
150–180 g/5½–6 oz.
   lobster meat or wild
   crayfish tails, freshly
   cooked
4 flour tortillas
25 g/1 cup baby salad
   leaves with herbs
lemon wedges, to serve

Guacamole
1 ripe avocado
1 tablespoon lime juice
1 tomato, deseeded and
   finely chopped
1 garlic clove, crushed
1 spring onion/scallion,
   finely chopped
1 tablespoon fresh
   coriander/cilantro,
   chopped
½ teaspoon chilli/chili
   powder
salt and freshly ground
   black pepper
lemon wedges, to serve

Serves 4

In Ian Fleming's novel *Goldfinger*, we read about Bond appreciating stone crabs; in *Casino Royale* he orders an avocado pear. What recipe could be more apt when viewing both of these films?

To make the guacamole, cut the avocado in half, remove the stone/pit and peel. Mash the flesh in a bowl with the lime juice, then stir in the tomato, garlic, spring onion/scallion, coriander/cilantro and chilli/chili powder. Season with salt and freshly ground black pepper. Mix the mayonnaise, Tabasco and sun-dried tomato paste together in a bowl. If using lobster, chop the meat into bite-sized pieces. Add the lobster or crayfish tails to the bowl and mix together. Lay the tortillas out on a clean work surface and top each one with the guacamole, baby salad leaves and shellfish cocktail. Roll each wrap tightly and cut in half. Serve with lemon wedges.

Diamonds are Forever Steak

Some might say that Bond only has one thing on his mind. But, as he proves in the *Diamonds Are Forever* novel when he confides to Tiffany Case that his ideal woman can 'make sauce béarnaise as well as love', he actually has two things on his mind: sex and food.

2–3 rib-eye steaks, about 225 g/8 oz. each and
2.5 cm/1 inch thick
olive oil, for rubbing
Béarnaise sauce
a handful of tarragon sprigs, leaves chopped,
   stalks reserved
3 tablespoons white wine vinegar
1 small shallot, chopped

6 black peppercorns
1 bay leaf
200 g/1¾ sticks unsalted butter
2 egg yolks
sea salt
lightly dressed watercress salad, to serve
ridged stove-top griddle/grill pan
Serves 2–3

First, prepare the base for the béarnaise sauce. Put the tarragon stalks in a saucepan and add the vinegar, shallot, peppercorns and bay leaf. Bring to the boil, then simmer until you have 1 tablespoon of liquid left. Strain into a small bowl and let cool. To cook the steaks, heat a ridged stove-top griddle/grill pan over high heat until almost smoking. Trim the steaks of any excess fat, pat dry with kitchen paper/paper towels, then rub a little oil into both sides. Add them to the pan and cook for 2–3 minutes, depending whether you want them rare or medium-rare. When you see spots of blood rise to the surface, turn them over and cook on the other side for another 1½–2½ minutes. Transfer to a warm plate and cover lightly with foil.

To make the béarnaise sauce, put the butter in a small saucepan and heat gently until melted. Skim off any white residue that floats to the surface, then bring almost to boiling point. Put the egg yolks in a food processor, add half the reduced vinegar and blend until the mixture begins to thicken. With the motor running, add the melted butter to the egg yolks very gradually. Once it begins to thicken, pour in the remaining butter in a steady stream. Stop pouring once you get to the milky residue at the bottom of the pan. Add the remaining reduced vinegar and a little salt and blend. Add the tarragon leaves and pulse to incorporate. Taste and adjust the seasoning. Serve the steaks with the sauce spooned over the top.

Russian Doll Cookies

These cute cookies should be served while *From Russia With Love* plays. Just like the film, these traditional dolls have many levels. But, unlike the film, they have nothing to do with explosions, belly dancers, getaway boat chases and coding machines.

700 g/1 lb. 9 oz. ready-made vanilla or gingerbread cookie dough
1 kg/2¼ lbs. royal icing mix
150–200 ml/⅔–¾ cup water
red and black food colourings
pink and white heart and star sugar sprinkles

2 baking sheets, lined with parchment paper
small piping bag with a small, round nozzle/tip
mini palette knife or small knife
Makes about 8–10 depending on size

Roll out the cookie dough on a lightly floured work surface. Cut out Russian doll shapes using a small, sharp knife. Arrange them on the prepared baking sheets. Refrigerate for 15 minutes. Preheat the oven to 180°C (350°F) Gas 4. Bake the cookies on the middle shelf of the preheated oven for about 12 minutes, or until firm. Let cool on the sheets for about 10 minutes before transferring to a wire rack to cool completely. Put the royal icing mix in a bowl and add the water gradually to form a thick, smooth paste. Divide between 3 bowls. Tint one red and one black using the food colourings. Leave the third bowl of icing white. Fill

the piping bag with whichever colour you want to start with. Pipe borders around the cold cookies. If you want to make the belly of the doll in the other colour of icing, you will need to create a border for this too. Flood the area inside the borders with icing: once you have made a neat border, you can spoon icing within the borders and spread it carefully up to the edges with a mini palette knife or small knife. Let dry. Pipe in the rest of the design and the dolls' faces. Pipe small flowers, dots, squiggles and whatever you like over the dolls, to decorate. Arrange the shaped sugar sprinkles all over and allow to set before serving.

Bollywood

'Cooking is the greatest art in the world' –
Cheeni Kum

Bollywood is perceived as producing all-singing, all-dancing extravaganzas that light up the screen. While this is often true, the Indian film industry also creates thought-provoking and provocative movies like *Dor* and *Mirch Masala*. You don't strictly have to show 'Indian' movies though; you could screen films with Indian characters, themes and, indeed, food… *Bend It Like Beckham, Bhaji On The Beach, Slumdog Millionaire*… To transport your guests to India, decorate the room with bright, rich colours – think vivid pink, green, blue, red, orange, purple and gold. You could buy Indian patterns from a fabric shop and use them for tablecloths, throws and drapes. Consider using banana leaves on your plates and platters, or as placemats to serve your dishes. Indian music could also be played before or after the films – people may even be inspired to make up their own dances, especially if they are wearing traditional Indian dress such as saris or sherwanis. However you decorate, whatever recipes you opt for, one thing's for sure: your guests are in for a night of delightful spice.

IT'S SHOWTIME!
Salaam Bombay!, Dil Chahta Hai, Cheeni Kum, Luv Shuv Tey Chicken Khurana, Mirch Masala, Mango Soufflé, Paheli, Mr India, Golmaal Film Series, Dor, 3 Idiots, Bobby, Slumdog Millionaire, Coolie, Fanaa, Fashion, Devdas, Baazigar, Taal, Jab We Met, Om Shanti Om, Bend It Like Beckham, Monsoon Wedding, Bride & Prejudice, Bawarchi.

Bombay Popcorn

Watch (and munch) as young Krishna finds himself in Bombay (now Mumbai) and has to fend for himself in *Salaam Bombay!* Your heart will go out to this down-on-his-luck lad as he navigates thieves, drug dealers and prostitutes.

1–2 tablespoons sunflower or vegetable oil

90 g/⅓ cup popcorn kernels

60 g/4½ tablespoons ghee (clarified butter)

1 tablespoon onion/nigella seeds

1 tablespoon dried curry leaves

1 generous tablespoon lime pickle

1 generous tablespoon mango chutney

Makes 1 large bowl

Heat the oil in a large lidded saucepan with a few popcorn kernels in the pan. When you hear the kernels pop, carefully tip in the rest of the kernels. Shake the pan over the heat until the popping stops. Take care when lifting the lid, as any unpopped kernels may still pop from the heat of the pan. Tip the popcorn into a bowl, removing any unpopped kernels as you go. Melt the ghee in a small saucepan set over low heat. Add the onion/nigella seeds and curry leaves and cook for a few minutes to flavour the oil. Add the pickle and chutney and cook for a few more minutes to heat through. Pour the spiced ghee over the popcorn and stir well so the kernels are evenly coated. Serve warm or cold.

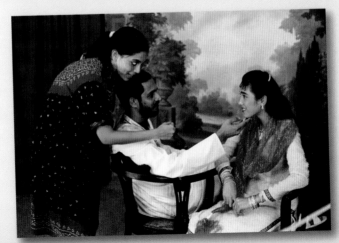

Rose Petal Drink

While this thirst-quencher won't appear with a click of the fingers – as the rose petals surrounding Lachchi in *Paheli* do – it won't take long to mix up this sweet, floral drink.

250 ml/1 cup coconut water or apple juice
125 ml/½ cup sugarcane juice or apple juice
1 teaspoon honey (optional)
a dash of rosewater
petals from 1 rosebud
freshly grated coconut (optional)
Serves 2

Chill all the ingredients except the rose petals or coconut. Put the coconut water and sugarcane juice or apple juice – in a jug/pitcher. Add the rosewater and honey to taste. Stir well and serve, sprinkled with rose petals. If preferred, you can add a little grated fresh coconut, and serve the drink in glasses half-filled with ice. This makes an impressive cocktail for non-drinkers.

Mango Chutney

Serve up this spicy mango chutney with mini poppadoms as a tasty appetizer as you watch *Slumdog Millionaire*. Your guests won't be able to stomach a large curry until after they find out whether Jamal has won the million!

1 tablespoon sunflower oil

1 teaspoon finely grated fresh ginger

2 garlic cloves, crushed

5 cloves

1 star anise

2 cassia barks or cinnamon sticks

5 black peppercorns

1–2 tablespoons nigella/onion seeds

½ teaspoon mild or medium chilli/chili powder

800 g/1¾ lbs. ripe but firm mango flesh, roughly chopped

400 ml/1⅔ cups white wine vinegar

270 g/1⅓ cup sugar

sea salt

mini poppadoms, to serve

Makes about 500 ml/2 cups

Heat the sunflower oil in a saucepan over medium heat. Add the ginger, garlic, cloves, star anise, cassia, peppercorns, nigella/onion seeds and chilli/chili powder and stir-fry for 1–2 minutes. Add the mango, vinegar and sugar and bring to the boil. Reduce the heat to low and cook for 45 minutes or until the mixture is jam-like. Season with sea salt to taste and serve with mini poppadoms, for dipping. You can preserve in hot, sterilized jars if not serving straightaway.

Spinach Dal

'I was married at your age... You don't even want to learn how to cook dal,' raged Jess's overbearing mother in Bend It Like Beckham. Luckily for your guests, they don't have to learn how to make dal, either – they'll score a tasty serving from you.

120 g/⅔ cup dried black lentils
40 g/3 tablespoons butter
1 onion, finely chopped
3 garlic cloves, crushed
2 teaspoons finely grated
   fresh ginger
2 green chillies/chiles, halved
   lengthways
1 teaspoon ground turmeric
1 teaspoon paprika
1 tablespoon ground coriander

1 tablespoon ground cumin
200-g/7-oz. can red kidney
   beans, drained and rinsed
200 g/7 oz. baby
leaf spinach
a large handful of fresh
   coriander/cilantro
   leaves, chopped
150 ml/⅔ cup double/
   heavy cream
Serves 4

Rinse the lentils. Drain, put them in a deep bowl and cover with cold water. Leave to soak for 10–12 hours. Rinse the lentils, then place in a saucepan with 500 ml/2 cups boiling water. Bring to the boil, reduce the heat and simmer for 35–40 minutes or until tender. Drain and set aside. Melt the butter in a saucepan and stir-fry the onion, garlic, ginger and chillies/chiles for 5–6 minutes, then add the turmeric, paprika, ground coriander, cumin, kidney beans and lentils. Add 500 ml/2 cups water and bring to the boil. Reduce the heat and stir in the spinach. Cook gently for 10–15 minutes, stirring often. Stir in the coriander/cilantro and cream.

Goan Shrimp Curry

Dil Chahta Hai is a wonderful tale of love, life and the beautiful beaches of Goa. Follow Akash, Sameer and Sid while diving into this curry and cringe/cry as romantic disaster strikes again and again.

2 tablespoons sunflower oil

2 onions, finely chopped

1 tablespoon finely grated fresh ginger

4 garlic cloves, crushed

2 red chillies/chiles, thinly sliced

¼ teaspoon ground turmeric

2 teaspoons ground coriander

1 teaspoon medium or hot chilli/chili powder

2 teaspoons ground cumin

1 tablespoon tamarind paste

200 ml/¾ cup coconut milk

1 teaspoon jaggery or dark brown sugar

1 kg/2¼ lbs. uncooked tiger prawns/jumbo shrimp, shelled and deveined but tails left intact

freshly chopped coriander/cilantro, to garnish

lime wedges, to serve

Serves 4

Heat the sunflower oil in a large saucepan and add the onions. Cook over medium heat for 4–5 minutes or until softened. Add the ginger, garlic and chillies/chiles and stir-fry for 1–2 minutes. Add the turmeric, ground coriander, chilli/chili powder and cumin and stir-fry for 1–2 minutes. Add the tamarind paste and coconut milk along with 300 ml/1¼ cups water and bring to the boil. Add the jaggery, reduce the heat to low and simmer gently for 15–20 minutes. Add the prawns/shrimp to the pan and cook over high heat for 4–5 minutes or until they turn pink and are cooked through. Season and remove from the heat. Garnish with the coriander/cilantro. Serve with lime wedges, steamed basmati rice and poppadoms.

Lemon Rice & Coconut Rice

If it weren't for a rice dish, Buddhadev and Nina would never have found love in *Cheeni Kum*. Got two friends you think would hit it off? Perhaps your movie night is the perfect time to play Cupid...

Lemon rice

225 g/1¼ cups basmati rice, rinsed

1 tablespoon light olive oil

12–14 fresh curry leaves

1 dried red chilli/chile

2 cassia barks or cinnamon sticks

2–3 cloves

4–6 cardamom pods, bruised

2 teaspoons cumin seeds

¼ teaspoon ground turmeric

juice of 1 large lemon

500 ml/2 cups boiling water

salt and freshly ground black pepper

Serves 4

Put the rice in a bowl, cover with cold water and let soak for 15 minutes. Drain thoroughly. Heat the olive oil in a non-stick saucepan and add the spices. Stir-fry for 20–30 seconds, then add the rice. Stir-fry for 2 minutes, then add the lemon juice and boiling water. Season and bring to the boil. Cover the pan reduce the heat to low and cook for 10–12 minutes. Let stand for 10 minutes. Fluff the rice with a fork and season.

Coconut rice

225 g/1¼ cups basmati rice, rinsed, soaked and drained (see above)

2 tablespoons sunflower oil

2 teaspoons black mustard seeds

2 teaspoons cumin seeds

2 dried red chillies/chiles

10 fresh curry leaves

500 ml/2 cups hot water

4 tablespoons coconut cream

2 tablespoons freshly grated coconut, to garnish

Serves 4

Heat the sunflower oil in a heavy-based saucepan and add tall the spicess. Stir-fry for 30 seconds, then add the hot water and the coconut cream. Stir well and bring to the boil. Reduce the heat to low, cover and cook for 10 minutes. Let stand for 10 minutes.

Fluff the rice with a fork and scatter over the grated coconut.

Chicken Tikka Masala

If you decide to screen *Luv Shuv Tey Chicken Khurana* while serving this curry, tell guests that the dish is actually called 'Chicken Khurana', and you are the genius who recovered the secret recipe, much to Omi's delight.

4 boneless, skinless chicken breasts, cut into
   bite-sized pieces
salt and freshly ground black pepper
freshly chopped coriander/cilantro leaves,
   to garnish
sliced red chillies/chiles, to garnish (optional)
Chicken tikka marinade
250 g/1 cup plain yogurt
1 tablespoon lemon juice
2 teaspoons ground cumin
1 teaspoon ground cinnamon
2 teaspoons cayenne pepper
2 teaspoons freshly ground
   black pepper

1 tablespoon finely
   grated fresh ginger
Masala sauce
15 g/1 tablespoon
   butter
1 garlic clove, crushed
1 red chilli/chile, finely chopped
2 teaspoons ground cumin
3 teaspoons paprika
200 g/7 oz. canned chopped tomatoes
2 tablespoons tomato purée/paste
200 ml/¾ cup double/heavy cream
warm naan or basmati rice, to serve
Serves 4

To make the chicken tikka marinade, combine all the ingredients in a large bowl and season with salt. Stir in the chicken, cover and refrigerate for 4–6 hours or overnight. Thread the marinated chicken onto metal skewers, discarding the marinade. Cook under a hot, preheated grill/broiler for about 5 minutes on each side. Meanwhile, make the tikka masala sauce. Melt the butter in a large, heavy-based frying pan over medium heat. Sauté the garlic and chilli/chile for 1 minute. Add the cumin and paprika and season well with salt and pepper. Purée the canned tomatoes in a blender until smooth, then add to the pan with the tomato purée/paste and the cream. Simmer over low heat for about 20 minutes until sauce has thickened. Add the grilled chicken to the pan and simmer for 10 minutes or until cooked through. Transfer to a serving platter and garnish with the coriander/cilantro and chillies/chiles, if using. Serve with warm naan or steamed basmati rice.

Mango Kulfi

2.25 litres/2½ quarts milk
180 g/¾ cup (caster) sugar
800 g/4 cups diced fresh
   ripe Alphonso mango
   flesh (about 6–8
   mangoes)
1 teaspoon orange flower
   water
black seeds from 20
   green cardamom pods
finely chopped pistachios
   and almonds, to serve
8 small ramekins, cups or
kulfi moulds
Serves 8

The mango is the national fruit of India, so you really could serve this tropical frozen dessert with any film from this genre. But if you want to get specific, *Mango Soufflé* – promoted as the first openly male gay film from India – would be a top choice.

Pour the milk into a large, wide, heavy-based saucepan and bring to the boil, stirring often. Simmer, stirring every 15 minutes, for 3–4 hours or until the volume has reduced to about 750 ml/3 cups and the milk is thick and dense. Stir in the sugar, then cool the pan and its contents in iced water. Stir in the mango flesh, orange flower water and cardamom seeds. Put into a blender and purée, in batches, until smooth. Stir well, pour into ramekins, cups or kulfi moulds and fast-freeze for 4–5 hours or until firm. When ready to unmould, chill in the fridge for 20 minutes, or dip briefly in cool water. To serve them the Indian way, cut a deep cross in the top of the turned-out kulfi so they thaw evenly. Serve, sprinkled with chopped pistachios and almonds.

Index